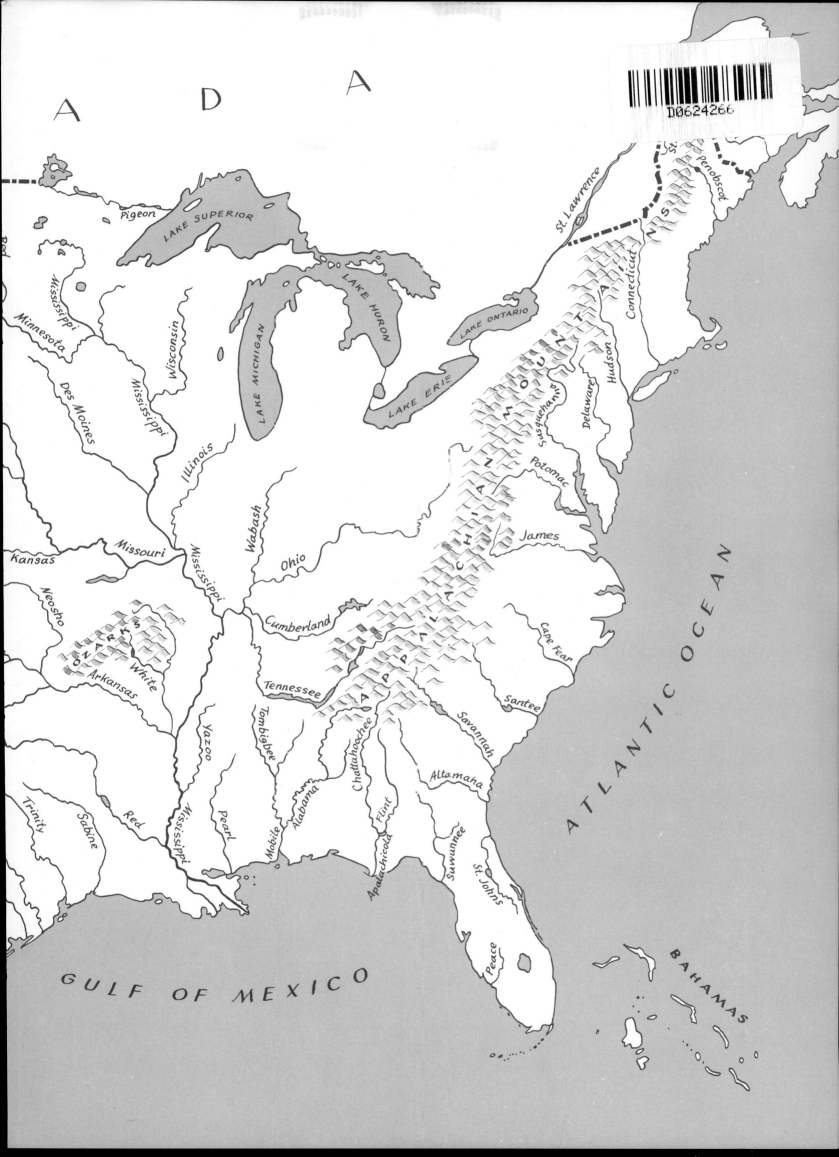

A   D   A

Pigeon

LAKE SUPERIOR

Red

Mississippi

Minnesota

Des Moines

Mississippi

Wisconsin

LAKE MICHIGAN

LAKE HURON

LAKE ONTARIO

LAKE ERIE

St. Lawrence

Penobscot

M O U N T A I N S

Connecticut

Hudson

Delaware

Susquehanna

Potomac

Illinois

Wabash

Ohio

Kansas

Missouri

Neosho

Mississippi

James

A P P A L A C H I A N

Cumberland

Cape Fear

Arkansas

White

Tennessee

Santee

Yazoo

Tombigbee

Savannah

Altamaha

ATLANTIC OCEAN

Trinity

Sabine

Red

Mississippi

Pearl

Mobile

Alabama

Chattahoochee

Flint

Apalachicola

Suwannee

St. Johns

Peace

BAHAMAS

GULF OF MEXICO

AMERICAN RIVERS

Bill Thomas

AMERICAN RIVERS
A Natural History

Special Consultant: **Dr. H. B. N. Hynes,** University of Waterloo

Designed by: **Philip Sykes**

Maps by: **Anne Marie Jauss**
Special Research Assistant: **Phyllis M. Thomas**

W. W. Norton & Company, Inc.

Other Books by Bill Thomas:

Tripping in America: Off the Beaten Track (1974)

Eastern Trips & Trails (1975)

Mid-America Trips & Trails (1975)

The Swamp (1976)

Lakeside Recreation Areas (1977)

The Complete World of Kites (1977)

The Ohio River Catalogue (1978)

First published, 1978, in the United States of America by W.W. Norton & Company, Inc. Published simultaneously in Canada by George J. McLeod Limited, Toronto.

First Edition

All rights reserved under International and Pan-American Copyright Conventions. Printed and bound by Dai Nippon Printing Co., Ltd., Tokyo, Japan

ISBN 0 393 08838 3

1 2 3 4 5 6 7 8 9 0

CONTENTS

To David and to friends of the river everywhere

ACKNOWLEDGMENTS

Production of such a book as *American Rivers* is seldom possible without the assistance of many individuals who devote considerable time and effort, many without further payment than the self-satisfaction of dedicating themselves to something in which they believe. *American Rivers* has been so ordained, and the author would like to express here a heartfelt thanks to those persons, including Dr. H.B.N. Hynes, a leading limnologist and biologist, member of the faculty at the University of Waterloo, Ontario, Canada; Dr. Frank Young and Dr. Don Whitehead of Indiana University; Dr. Thomas F. Waters of the University of Minnesota; Dr. Phil Greeson, U.S. Geological Survey; Adele and the late Lloyd Beesley of Cedar Grove, Indiana; John Ebeling of Lake Hubert, Minnesota; Wendell Metzen of Waycross, Georgia, and Tom Telfer, wildlife biologist of the Hawaii Division of Fish & Game on Kauai.

Dr. C. E. Cushing of Pacific Northwest Laboratories, Washington; Virginia Carter, U.S. Geological Survey; Dr. N. H. Anderson of Oregon State University; Dr. E. F. Benfield of Virginia Polytechnic Institute; Dr. John Bozeman, Ms. Jingle Davis and Barry Vaughn of the Georgia Dept. of Natural Resources; Dr. Gene Likens of Cornell University; Dr. Richard Baumann of Brigham Young University; Dr. Andrew Sheldon of the University of Montana; Bill Thomas of the Alaska Field Office, Bureau of Outdoor Recreation; Bob Nagel of Valentine, Nebraska; Nancy Perkin of Harrisburg, Pennsylvania; Dr. Suzanne and Larry Prather, Lincoln, Nebraska; Professor Lee Jenkins, Columbia, Missouri; Nancy Erb of the Sierra Club; Dennis Wolkoff of The Nature Conservancy; Danny Muldrew of Lucasville, Ohio; and to Phyllis, Alan, and Billy for their unlimited assistance in producing the research, photographs, and organization in this work.

To my editors—Starling Lawrence and Jim Mairs—a special thanks for without them, this book would never have become a reality.

INTRODUCTION
THE RIVER

Nothing in the universe exists alone.
Every drop of water, every human being, all creatures
in the web of life and all ideas in the web
of knowledge, are part of an immense, evolving,
dynamic whole as old—and as young—as
the universe itself. To learn this is
to discover the meaning of joy.
—David Cavagnaro/*This Living Earth*

*1. A healthy river is a remarkable part of earth's
complete ecosystem. Each year, they become fewer
and fewer. This one—the Eleven Point—is located in
the Missouri Ozarks.*

Before there was man, there was the river. It preceded the mountains, the trees and virtually all other forms of life. A healthy river, in its natural condition, is a complete ecosystem, vibrant with energy and life. It is a vital link to creation, to the longevity of the planet Earth. Without it, our society—indeed, all living things—would perish.

Rivers are born not of the earth but of the heavens. They begin, as life begins, with a simple particle. A raindrop is shed from a passing cloud, and the miracle is conceived. How many raindrops are counted in the age of a stream, or in a single moment's flow? The drops are the beginning, the heaving restless oceans the end. And then the cycle starts anew. The open seas, unprotected from the direct rays of the sun, evaporate into the skies to again energize the river.

There is evidence that rivers are cosmic; traces of them have been found on other planets. Early aerial surveys of Mars, for example, show what appears to be a latticework of dry stream beds. How, or when, they were created has not yet been determined. There are even rivers within our own oceans. The Gulf Stream actually could be termed a great river within the Atlantic, measuring roughly fifty miles wide and two thousand feet deep. It flows constantly north along the U.S. Coast, then dissipates in the Atlantic as it heads generally toward Europe. Its current travels approximately five to six miles an hour. At certain points, such as along the South Carolina coast, it separates—not unlike a braided Arctic river in Alaska—and flows as several much slower streams some six hundred feet deep with an aggregate width of 150 miles.

The ocean actually is filled with interesting rivers. In 1952, a submarine river 250 miles wide, known as the Cromwell current, was discovered flowing eastward three hundred feet below the surface of the Pacific Ocean for 3,500 miles along the equator. Its volume is one thousand times that of the Mississippi. Unlike other rivers, these rivers of the ocean gain much of their energy from difference in water temperatures and the rotation of the planet, and they have a dramatic impact upon climate.

Since the earth was born, two mighty forces have shaped the land: the movement of the earth's crust that pushes mountains up, and erosion on its surface that has worn the land away. The principal instrument of erosion is water. Whether in a great glacier or flowing between the banks of a river, water has the final say about the shape of the land.

The river, some contend, is the greatest single persistent force on earth. Even the inner volcanic forces which sporadically shatter the planet cannot match the continuous force of flowing water. Contain the water and it will fill its container, seek out the lowest and weakest point, and overflow. Once it begins to overflow, it begins to cut away, to wear down, to grind and tumble and wash away the material that seeks to restrain it. The process is timeless, the result certain. Even the great dams built to harness and control virtually every stream in America today—were they not constantly and properly maintained at great taxpayer expense—would eventually crumble before the thrust of the river.

2

3

2. *Grindelia, sometimes called tarweed, are found in some river valleys where there's moist soil.*

3. *Rivers are excellent habitat for many types of wildlife, from the smallest cocoon to the great Canada goose which nests along them.*

4. *What can be more beautiful than a lazy midwestern stream on a tranquil autumn day? The leaves begin to fall, providing new energy as they decay.*

6

7

5. Most rivers are born at higher elevations, many as little brooks. As they travel, they gather the waters from other little brooks and tributary streams, carrying it all like a great artery to the ocean. This brook is on the author's Indiana woodland.

6. The birthplace of a river is often found where ferns grow, deep in the shaded damp woodlands. Here the rains seep into the soil to escape elsewhere as springs.

7. Clusters of deadly amanita mushrooms are found along some river valleys. Most wet, wooded areas are good producers of mushrooms.

8. (Overleaf) In dry lands relatively unprotected from rains, even small streams may soon cut impressive canyons, as the Palouse River has done in eastern Washington.

The river is always restless. Even in its gentle moods, it is hungry, forever tugging at whatever is within reach, lapping at the shores, undermining the banks that would contain it and give it direction and bearing. That which is beyond reach is safe only for the day; tomorrow the river will rise to set it adrift and carry it away. Anything untethered to the earth along its banks belongs to the river tomorrow or the next day. The permanent or tethered things may stay put until next year or next century. But they, too, will eventually become a part of the river.

The variety of rivers is in direct correlation to the variety of climates and earth surfaces. The desert is full of rivers without water; they flow only after heavy rains, become raging torrents within minutes, and in the next hour, vanish again. Always following the path of least resistance, rivers tumble over hard rock, cut through soft rock, meander across broad earthen flood plains. In their currents they carry the material of the continents from one place to another, building broad delta fans, a sandbar here, a gravelbar there.

The names of running water are many: river, stream, creek, brook, rivulet, freshet, arroyo, bayou, slough, rill, burn, and runnel. And while some differentiations are made according to volume, or size, the number of names in various geographical regions of the nation indicate how many different characters running water can take. In some places, the names are interchangeable; some creeks are called rivers, some rivers creeks.

Whatever its shape or size, the sound of the river is music to the ears. From the frolicsome snow-melt brook cutting across an alpine meadow to the bulging, lazy river winding under a noonday summer sun, there is a poetry to the movement of water across and through the land. Where the gradient is steep, the velocity is great, cutting quickly to bedrock, pausing only to fill a basin or lose itself in a pond choked with green growing things and teeming aquatic life. Young water is noisy water; the larger, older rivers grow quiet and talk little, their secrets locked deep within them. In distance and in time, they become barely audible.

Each river is born with the singular task of reducing the terrain through which it flows to a sea-level plain; the degree to which this job has been completed is the measure of its relative age. Thus, in its youth a river will cut deeply and vigorously, forming sharp, V-shaped canyons, creating many rapids and gathering unto itself many tumbling tributaries. In its middle age, a river will have created broad, U-shaped valleys where there once had been canyons, and it will flow much more slowly and gently. By old age, its work nearly done, a river will meander sluggishly through a valley that has become so broad as to be hardly noticeable.

On the surface, the river appears simple, yet it is complex with many dimensions. Life's profusion and diversity are both accommodated and encouraged in the stream's environment. Every meter is utilized: living things exist on its surface, send root to the cozy bottom, release eggs to its current, retrieve them to eat.

The river is actually a composite of many habitats, from rapids to waterfalls to sluggish stretches and placid backwaters. Yet it is constant in one way; the **13** water is always on the move. To survive in this ever-changing world, plants and animals have had to adapt their structure and habits in many ways. Some animals, such as fishes, are streamlined like airplanes. As a result, trout and other fishes are able to make their way upstream or hold their position against a strong current. Many insects, such as certain mayfly nymphs, are also streamlined.

On the other hand, many aquatic creatures are not streamlined; their bodies have not adapted to the flow of water, and thus they must struggle against the force of the current or avoid it entirely. They choose the latter whenever possible. Some hide beneath rocks. Others burrow in the bottom. The net-winged midge larvae cling to rocks with powerful suction cups; some creatures depend on stout claws, hooks, or gluelike secretions to keep them from being swept downstream.

The river is alive with activity every hour of the day. An entire community, more bustling than Manhattan during rush hour, exists in every cubic foot of the stream. How to get oxygen from the water, how to snatch food as it passes by in the current, how to find a mate and reproduce more of its kind—these processes are repeated continuously in the river. And because each stream is distinctly different, each presents its own set of life-or-death challenges and criteria to the creatures who live in it. Forever posing new problems of survival, the river is never an easy place for life. But its community of animals and plants is always rich, varied, and endlessly fascinating.

And at the base of it all is a water molecule. David Cavagnaro, in *Living Water,* describes these watery adventures of the molecule, which is indestructible and eternal:

> What wondrous stories a water molecule could tell of wild peaks visited on stormy nights, of quiet rivulets and raging rivers traveled, of peaceful fogs and sun-colored clouds, of glaciers and ocean currents, of fragile snowflakes and crisp little frost crystals, and of the seething protoplasmic retorts of living cells—a zillion places visited since the earth's beginning.

The survival of the complex aquatic communities depends upon the speed of the current, climate, and composition of the streambed. At the top of the riverine food chain are hundreds of species of fish; below them are arrayed minnows, snails, leeches, worms, clams, mussels, crustaceans, insects and their larvae, plants, moss, and algae. Because its medium is motion, the river's ecosystem is one of the most difficult to analyze and protect. It is also one of the most fragile; each action upon the river or against it results in some counteraction or effect.

During the summer the river grows warmer, and the farther it flows from its source, the warmer it gets. Since various life forms can survive only within a certain temperature range, the sun's rays play a great role in the type of creatures found living in the river's various segments.

The flow or volume of a river also is responsive to the seasons. As soon as the trees are in full leaf in the spring, the depth of the river, barring unusually heavy rains, may drop. That's because so much water normally flowing into the stream now is taken up by trees and green growing things and transpired through their leaves into the atmosphere. Consequently, it never gets to the river. Even water plants take liquid from the river and transpire it into the air.

Photosynthesis, of course, is the key to life. The river microcosm, and indeed the whole living world, obtains the energy for its basic existence, its activities, and its maintenance from the photosynthetic process. Through photosynthesis the sun's energy is transformed into food—into micro-algae in the stream, into grasses in the field. These organisms are in turn the producers of nutrition for themselves as well as others. Food energy is transferred through a succession of different animals eating and being eaten—this makes up the food chain. Man's place is at the uppermost position of the chain. He eats the fish that eats the nymph that eats the plant that produces nourishment through the sun's radiant energy. And when man dies, his remains are consumed by the tiny life forms at the bottom of the chain, thus completing the cycle.

The river taps into the land to enrich the lives of the creatures that live within it. And the land, so often thirsty, taps the river for drink. The relationship between the two is one of great intimacy. Many land organisms are tied to river ecosystems and cannot survive without them. A salamander enters the quiet pools of the backwater to lay its eggs. Many types of insects do likewise. The eggs then become food for some forms of life in the river; some eggs survive to hatch, producing nymphs which, in turn, also are eaten by other life forms. Some of the nymphs survive to maturity, however, and the insects they produce rise to the surface of the water and fly, swim, or crawl away.

The river provides moisture for parched landscapes such as the deserts and the prairies. That moisture spurs the growth of trees along the banks, which provide cooling shelter for the river, allowing it to support life forms that could not otherwise survive the high water temperatures. It is part of nature's own air-conditioning and cooling system.

Then comes the end of the hot season, the trees shed their leaves, and winds break twigs, which fall into the water. These add to the river's fertility. As they drift, they become saturated with water and sink to the bottom, where they become a type of compost. As they decay, they provide habitat and energy for other life forms. And the river becomes a more fertile place.

Dr. H. B. N. Hynes of the University of Waterloo, one of the world's leading stream limnologists, points out in his book *The Ecology of Running Waters* how important a role the leaf plays in energizing the stream. "Fallen leaves are quite a good foodstuff in their own right," he says. "Elm leaves contain 7.5 per cent of their air-dried weight in the form of protein. Other species of tree leaf have since been found to contain similar amounts..."

Plankton, mostly associated with lakes and still bodies of water, also plays a role in the ecosystem of rivers. So does algae. As algae forms, coating underwater rocks and logs with green and brown slimy carpets, long filaments may trail in the current. Occasion-

ally they break away, drift to new locations, and latch onto some other object. Never are they wasted; they become part of the river's food web. Mosses play a role, too. A thick mat of moss on a boulder may be home for thousands of tiny animals—water bears, insects, mites, scuds, rotifers. In quieter waters are cattails and lilies which are shelter, security, and home to many creatures seeking a quieter place to live out the main flow of the river.

Usually the more densely wooded the land through which a river flows, the more enriched the river's waters. The rain forest river is much more productive, generally speaking, than a desert or prairie river. In fact, ecologists have found that prairie rivers are relatively poor producers, mainly because they collect so little organic matter from the plants and trees. The contribution to the river by botanical growth is important. Not only does it include dead leaves, but flowers and fruit of trees and even the feces of land insects and animals, all adding to the river's food energy.

So the land does have a vital effect upon the river. And the river has a like effect upon the land. It even has a moderating influence upon the climate, ofttimes extending the range of both plants and animals. The Carolina wren is found far north of its range nesting on the cliffs of the Hudson River Palisades; other birds, wildflowers, insects live north of their normal range, too, just because of the river.

So the communities of creatures that comprise riverine life are indeed complex. They give the stream impetus and importance. For it is that complexity that makes the river function. A healthy river, for instance, does not suffer from pollution. It is a remarkable cleanser and given the opportunity will within a few miles break down and consume the waste of a fair-sized city. It's only when it becomes overburdened with too much waste, too much pollution, that it is no longer able to function. Moderation is the key; excesses it cannot tolerate, and since most rivers are targets of excesses, they are either dying or are dead. The tiny creatures, the plants that comb and filter the water, no longer survive. And with their demise also go the creatures that feed upon them and the creatures that feed upon those creatures. And, don't forget, man is also a part of that life chain.

The blockage of normal flow of a river greatly alters its ecosystem and does great damage as well. First of all, the dams raise the water level. This permits less sunlight to reach the bottom of the stream, eliminating altogether or seriously limiting the growth of such bacteria and minute creatures that depend upon energy from the sun. The dam also decreases the flow or current in the stream, seriously limiting the food gathering capability of those creatures that depend upon the current to deliver nutriment to them. Secondly, the slower current allows the water to drop the burden of silt and debris it carries. It builds up into a muddy ooze and sludge on the bottom, actually burying many of the small creatures that live there.

True, the raising of the water level often causes the river to spread over portions of its own valley—the immediate flood plain. Thus it provides greater space

9. As the river attempts to escape the high country, it may create waterfalls such as this one on Havasu Creek, a tributary of the Colorado River, in the Grand Canyon.

10. The New River's Sandstone Falls in West Virginia. The New, acclaimed as one of the most ancient rivers in North America, is a leftover from the mighty Teays which preceded the Mississippi and flowed generally north, not south.

11. Rivers which flow through V-shaped valleys are generally not as old as rivers with vast flood plains, such as the Mississippi. Shown here is the Snake River in Wyoming.

12. The seasons also are a part of the river; in fall the leaves turn and drop to the ground, where they decay, energizing the soil and the water that falls upon it and flows to the stream. They are charged with nutrients which support new life along the way, adding to the great ecosystem of the stream.

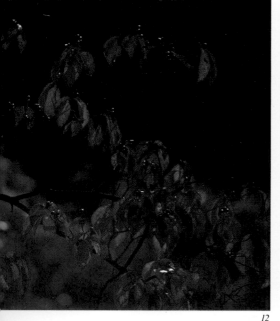

12

13. The river is an attraction for all kinds of wildlife; it provides habitat and perhaps even geographical guidance to migrating birds and waterfowl, such as these Canada geese heading south along the great Mississippi flyway.

13

and habitat for those creatures seeking quieter off-stream or out-of-the-current habitat. But it also places the stream on new land, which it immediately begins to erode. Usually the Corps of Engineers, before building a dam, will cut all timber from the area to be inundated, as well as close by areas where the river might flood. Consequently, there is nothing to hold the soil.

But the Corps is not concerned with biological adversities. Instead it thinks of navigation and flood control; the rest be damned. Only in recent times has it given lip service to the environment and only then to achieve public support for its own existence. Too many complaints from too many people have gotten through to the Congress, and the Corps has become the villain in the story of the rivers of America.

Fortunately, the public is more aware today than it has ever been of the important ecological role played by our rivers. That, indeed, is the purpose of this book. Its aim is to bring about a better awareness among people everywhere that the river is a vital part of the earth, that it needs to be preserved with as little change as possible. A small alteration by man may in fact become a critical one to the creatures of the riverine community. Even if man carried through with every possible measure to preserve the rivers, it might not be enough to compensate for the extra pressures wrought by the vastly increased human population. But there is hope; the Willamette River project engaged in by the people of Oregon is proof positive that rivers can be reclaimed from extinction.

Further proof was enacted by the U.S. Congress when in October 1968 the Wild and Scenic Rivers Act became law. Said the Congress:

It is hereby declared to be the policy of the United States that certain selected rivers of the Nation which, with their immediate environments, possess outstandingly remarkable scenic, recreational, geologic, fish and wildlife, historic, cultural, or other similar values, shall be preserved in free-flowing condition, and that they and their immediate environments shall be protected for the benefit and enjoyment of present and future generations. The Congress declares that the established national policy of dam and other construction at appropriate sections of the rivers of the United States needs to be complemented by a policy that would preserve other selected rivers or sections thereof in their free-flowing condition to protect the water quality of such rivers and to fulfill other vital national conservation purposes.

The Congress and the public in general has yet to consider that every river, regardless of its location or size, is vitally important to the survival of man. Indicator warnings—fish kills, cancer scares, the decimation of pelicans and other creatures—hint that man's casual mistreatment of the river may indeed produce dire circumstances at some time in the future. Already it is later than we think!

The water you wash your hands in today may indeed be the same water that Cleopatra bathed in centuries ago. But if we do not better protect and preserve the natural purifiers in the future than we have during the past hundred years, the water your children or grandchildren know may be toxic to touch. And it is difficult to visualize the survival of man in a world with only poisoned water.

14

16

15

17

20

18

19

14. *A stream, while often docile and beautiful, can also be quarrelsome and devastating. Here debris lodged along the banks of Colorado's Big Thompson Creek is a memorial to those who built too close to its banks and lost life and property in the flash flood of 1976.*

15. *Floods are a part of the natural character of a river. Though houses and roadways on the flood plain may be swept away, the trees shown here will suffer no lasting damage.*

16. *Big Thompson Creek, during the 1976 flash flood, completely changed the area through which it flows, creating new gravel bars and new channels.*

17. *Where the flood plain allows, the river spreads out, slowing down and dropping its debris and silt among trees and plant life which filter and clean the waters.*

18. *Raindrops on sassafras leaves: the beginning of a river.*

19. *Some rivers flood regularly; flooding is almost an annual occurrence on the Ohio, shown here at Louisville, Kentucky.*

20. *Big Thompson Creek played no favorites in cleaning out the canyon; here the waters swept out an asphalt highway within a two-hour period.*

1

OZARK
RIVERS

Everywhere there is a leafy sound
of rising, running, flowing.
If we should place our ears to the ground
we might hear the pulsing of a heart.
—Ward Dorrance/*Three Ozark Streams*

*1. Some people believe the Jack's Fork to be the
most beautiful stream of the
Missouri Ozarks.
It now is part of a national scenic waterway.*

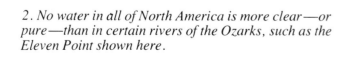

2. No water in all of North America is more clear—or pure—than in certain rivers of the Ozarks, such as the Eleven Point shown here.

Sandwiched between four distinctly different geographic regions in the midst of America is a relatively small area of honeycomb karst, huge sinkholes, ravenous caverns, and gushing springs, a land dissected by a lacework of beautiful clearwater streams. This geographical and geological gem is called the Ozarks. Generally conceded to be the oldest in North America, these mountains were not born of uplift or violent forces, but instead carved and worn away by water. Unquestionably it's one of the most unique areas on earth; so are its rivers.

The Ozarks cover some 55,000 square miles of white oak, sycamore, and pine forest in Missouri, Arkansas, Kansas, and Oklahoma. A newcomer to this area might not notice at first that these mountains are different. The tops are virtually all the same height.

Extending from the forests of southern Missouri just beyond St. Louis through northern Arkansas to the Oklahoma plains, the Ozarks are bounded by five major rivers—the Mississippi, the Missouri, the Osage, the Neosho, and the Arkansas.

Geologists will tell you that during the Paleozoic Era—400-500 million years ago—the Ozarks were covered by a vast inland sea. The waters deposited layers of sandstone and limestone, and when the water withdrew it left horizontal rocks—a tableland plateau. And then the rivers formed as rains fell, beginning an endless and tireless sculpture of the rock, until the land began to look old. The old Ozarks, strewn with old boulders, forested with trees gnarled and twisted and stunted as though with age, punctuated with rivers running clear as though they, too, are old and have long ago carried away the silt and soil that would have muddied their waters. The Ozarks are indeed old, everything about them.

"Our mountains ain't so high, but our valleys shore are deep," goes one Ozark expression. It fits, for the Ozarks could boast no peaks—not even hills—were it not for the valleys the rivers have gouged. Elevations here seem unremarkable beside even the Appalachians, much less the Rockies. Hoisting semaphores of dogwood and redbud in spring, consumed in the hot flame of oaks and gums and sassafras in autumn, a clutch of peaks called the Boston Mountains struggles up almost to 2,600 feet, the highest point in the Arkansas Ozarks. Missouri's highest peak, Taum Sauk Mountain, rises to 1,772 feet. But the ruggedness of the Ozarks does not derive from grand extremes; it comes from the wrinkled landscape's affinity for the vertical. What the hills lack in height they make up for in steepness.

Even the origin of the name has been lost somewhere in the past. Several theories persist. Some believe it was a French name for a tree from which the Indian took wood for their bows—the Osage orange or hedge apple. The French trappers who came to the area in the eighteenth century called this tree the Bois d'Arc. Indians and the first pioneers corrupted it to Ozarks. The area has always held a certain magic, even to the Osage Indians who for many years used it as a hunting preserve. But it was a white man—Henry R. Schoolcraft, amateur explorer, botanist, and adventurer from the East—who first described it. After months trekking **25**

3

4

3. The pockmarked cliffs caused by leaching waters over eons of time have become virtual trademarks of the Ozarks.

4. Limestone outcroppings, worn down by water through the ages, protrude along the banks of streams, a geologic reminder of the "old" Ozarks.

5. Black-eyed susans, cardinal flowers, and a score of other wildflowers provide a kaleidoscopic bouquet along Ozark streams during spring, summer, and fall.

6. Curled dock, a plant native to Europe, also grows along the Eleven Point River in the Ozarks.

7. Day lilies blooming in semishade along an Ozark stream.

through the Ozark , he felt it most resembled the Rhineland of Germany, and he wrote: "The Ozarks are a sort of Rheingau, through which the rivers burst."

One of those rivers bursting from the Ozark Mountains was a shining stream called by the French La Rivière Courante (Running Water). Schoolcraft anglicized it to "Current," and the name has stuck to this day. Although there are many streams in the Ozarks—the Black, the Eleven Point, the Gasconade, the Jacks Fork, the Buffalo, the Spring—the Current is perhaps the stream most associated with the region. It was the Current, combined with its tributary, Jacks Fork, after all, that became the first national scenic river. In August, 1964, Congress authorized the Ozark National Scenic Riverways, assuring preservation of 140 miles of clear, swift-flowing streams in southern Missouri, the first to be specifically preserved within the national park system for their own intrinsic values.

From the crevices of the Boston Mountains, past gnarled cedars clinging to sheer cliffs, wanders the Buffalo River, one of the most pleasant streams in the Ozarks, now also protected by the National Park Service. So untouched by man, it has become what the National Park Service calls one of the nation's most significant natural rivers. The Army Corps of Engineers planned to dam the Buffalo to prevent flooding in the 1950s, but were forced to call a halt to the project in the face of fierce opposition by environmentalists.

The streams of the Ozarks are remarkably clean. One reason for this purity is the chert rock (a dull-colored flintlike quartz found in limestone) and lush

8

8. *Watercress grows profusely among limestone boulders along the Current River.*

9. *Great sand and gravel bars are formed by Ozark streams at many places along their route, such as this one on the Black River.*

9

growths of water plants which make up their composite bed. Chert is perhaps the most common rock of the region. Harder than glass and sharp-edged, it was once prized by the Indians as a material for cutting tools. And it provides an excellent filter system, literally combing the waters of the streams as they flow along the chert floor. It is small, pear-shaped, and comes in several colors. Thickly embedded in many Ozark limestones and colomites, chert is almost insoluble in water. As logging and burning reduced the forest cover in years past and overgrazing thinned the soil, leaving it to the mercy of the forty-odd inches of rainfall here each year, the chert naturally was flushed into the streams . . . and that's where it stayed.

While the waters of Ozark streams are among the purest in the nation, this condition—because of the lack of bacteria—is not very conducive to plant life. While the streams do support a trout fishery, some bass and bluegill, they are not noted as great producers of fish. They are simply too clean. Still, there are occasional holes which have collected silt and are home to some whopper fish.

During the latter half of the nineteenth century, logging was mercilessly destructive to the Ozarks. The great trees that grew here, some predating the discovery of America, had considerable commercial value. With the construction of the transcontinental railroads, there was urgent need for railroad ties, and "tie-whacking," as it was called by the natives, became a major occupation. Thousands of miles of track were laid on ties from the Ozarks, most of them white oak. Other species— shortleaf pine, black oak, hickory, and black walnut—were in demand for other industries, too, and pretty soon the hills and hollows were stripped of the great trees. Sawdust piles, the only leftover reminders from the great mills, still dot the countryside.

By the turn of the century, there was little left but scrub forest. Traditional annual burning to clear the forest of undergrowth by the people who settled here—largely mountaineers from the Appalachians of Tennessee and Kentucky—finished off much of what was left. It was not until sometime later that the U.S. Forest Service stepped in, bought up large tracts of land, and created two national forests—the Clark and the Mark Twain—to restore the land and start it on the road to healthy timber production. Still the burning was carried on by the few natives left on the land; it continues a problem to this day.

Although a substantial amount of water falls each year on the Ozarks, the plant life it supports is not lush, for the water drains quickly through the porous limestone of the hills, down into fissures and enormous water-filled caves. Some valleys of the Ozarks in other places would be large enough to sustain noteworthy rivers; here they run dry year-round except immediately following a heavy rain. Most of the time their water runs underground.

It is the subterranean flow of water that is most remarkable in the Ozarks. So voluminous is it that many believe it originates far to the north, fed by great glaciers in Alaska and northern Canada. Others believe it originates under the Great Lakes. The truth, geologists say, is that it is only rainwater, filtered by the 29 karst. It is crystal clear, between fifty-five and sixty degrees throughout the year, and largely devoid of oxygen.

Springs abound throughout the Ozarks, some small, some huge, such as Big Springs on the Current River, one of the two largest single-outlet springs in North America. From it emerges nearly a billion gallons of water per day, enough to supply the entire water needs of New York City. At Blue Spring on the Current River, the pool is seventy-five feet across and clear enough for one to see forty feet down; the bottom is still another two hundred feet or more below that.

The porous rock of the Ozarks was formed by the rainwater filtering through decaying matter—leaves, rotting wood, grasses—charging the water with carbon dioxide. This chemically charged water ate away the more soluble portions of the limestone, leaving it pockmarked and honeycombed. Long continued solution by this slow alchemy ultimately produced large caverns, fissures, and channelways. Some three thousand caves have been discovered in Missouri, another 1,500 in the Arkansas portion of the Ozarks. Some have antechambers the size of cathedrals and extend twenty-five miles into the earth. Here, living without light on a food chain that begins with droppings from bats, are found blind white cavefish and pale blind salamanders.

Special communities of plant life have established themselves around the springs. More than fifty species of plant life—watercress, milfoil, starwort, needle spike rush, water speedwell, and waterweed as well as a variety of ferns and mosses—grow profusely under conditions provided by the stabilized water temperatures. Animal life is virtually nonexistent in the springs, but as the water flows over tumbling rocks, it soon gathers enough oxygen to tolerate limited generation of some microscopic forms and ultimately higher species of aquatic life.

The distinct boundaries of the Ozarks have isolated some of the region's plant and animal life. More than 160 species of fish are found here, thirteen of them unique to the Ozarks. More than 3,500 species of plants thrive here, and a goodly number of those, too, can be found at no other place.

The huge animals that once roamed these hills—elk, buffalo, panther, and bear—all have been wiped out by excessive hunting. The black bear, however, is making some comeback since the U.S. Forest Service took over thousands of acres. White-tailed deer are plentiful, and there is a respectable population of wild turkey, once nearly extinct here. More than one hundred species of butterfly are found here. The streams of the Ozarks provide an interesting study of subtle interactions in a shared environment. Various species of fish that share a single gravel bar for spawning await their turn as nature prescribes it. Some spawn a little earlier or a little later, a little bit deeper underwater or a little closer to the bank. The bleeding shiner even sneaks its eggs into the rocky nest built by the hornyhead chub.

The Ozarks is a unique wilderness—or, as some describe it, a half-wilderness. It bears the signs of man's use and abuse, but it has survived. And since it is losing population, it will probably return someday to full wilderness status.

10. *A rainy day on the Eleven Point River, now preserved by the U.S. Forest Service.*

11. *True watercress grows profusely along Ozark streams. One condition for its survival is pure, high-quality water.*

11

2

RIVERS
OF
THE NORTH
WOODS

It was beginning to be very wild and quiet.
I remembered to be frightened and right away I was.
It was the beautiful impersonality of the place
that struck me the hardest;
I would not have believed that it could hit me
all at once like this, or with such force.
The silence and the silence-sound of the river
had nothing to do with any of us.
—James Dickey

1. The Wolf River is born in the great evergreen forest.

Once it was a vast green belt of boreal forest extending from the southern fringes of the snowbelt all the way to the Arctic tundra. Its exact perimeters were ill defined, for the transition to other geographical territory was gradual. No one could mark the precise boundary where the North Woods began or ended. Today it is even less definable, for the land has been timbered, patches cleared, and resources tapped; but it generally covers a good part of an area geologists refer to as the Canadian Shield.

The North Woods in places are still dense, the soils sparse and rocky, the streams cold and clear. But the trees are mostly second growth; the mighty hemlocks, firs, and spruces are gone.

The streams of the North Woods belong to two watersheds—one rushing toward the St. Lawrence and the North Atlantic via the Great Lakes; the other down the Mississippi to the Gulf of Mexico. The Wisconsin River, meandering through Wisconsin from the evergreen forest of Michigan's Upper Peninsula, ultimately meets the Mississippi; the Fox, whose headwaters are only a mile away from the Wisconsin at one point, flows instead into Lake Michigan.

Playing a vital role in the character of these streams is the rugged climate. During winter, the North Woods are locked in a grip of snow and ice. The ponds and lakes freeze thickly, sometimes as much as four to six feet. The days are short, the nights long and bitterly cold. Herbaceous plants lie dead in all but their seeds or roots, and the trees seem frozen and lifeless. The white wilderness is quiet except for the winter nights, when you can hear the trees snap like rifles, as their fibers separate under pressure from extremely low temperatures. Only the tracks of a few animals and birds suggest the land still lives.

But then comes the spring—by late May—and the land blossoms; the bloodroot stirs and comes to life, pushing up through the mulch laid down by the decades of needles and leaves. A leaf bud swells with the sap pumped from the earth by a warm sun, and soon ferns and a thousand other plants are pushing upward through the forest floor. The migrating birds are back; the eagle soars overhead, its screams mingling with the shrill call of the pileated woodpecker, the soft sounds of the great barred owl, the forlorn cry of the loon. Swarms of mosquitoes and black flies emerge from the forest floor. Suddenly, after eight months of winter, the North Woods are vibrant with life.

These woods once were a gold mine as early explorers and lumberjacks came this way. Hardly an acre was not cut over, descendants of the trees that had stood since the retreat of the glacier during the Ice Age felled and floated down the rivers to sawmills. The rivers were important highways then; there were no others. The great stumps, tall as a man's head and broad enough to park a Volkswagen on, dot the landscape to this day, monuments to the giants that once stood there.

Once the timber was depleted, however, the woods were left alone. The rugged climate, lack of fertile soil, pesty insects that could drive a man virtually insane during the summer months all combined toward the preservation of the North Woods. And, gradually, the

34

3. The paperbark birch, a striking contrast to the deep green of the North Woods.

4. Crested dwarf iris.

Bill Deane

4

3

woodland recovered. Most of the rivers escaped being harnessed; there was little or no demand for the power they could produce. The people, the industry, the farms were elsewhere.

From the air, the North Woods looks like a plain dotted with innumerable lakes and potholes. During summer the bare knobs of pink granite offer stark contrast to the green in the hollows and the dark swirls of the marshes. During winter the forests stand out as though sketched with charcoal. But the colors are cold and sometimes stark and harsh; the softness of warmer climes is seldom seen here.

To understand this region, one must take a good look at its geology. Between 3.6 and 2.5 billion years ago, the oldest shield rocks formed. They were once lavas and sedimentary rocks. Mountain-building so heated and squeezed them that they recrystalized completely. Between these granites of the oldest regions lie many narrow, sinuous belts of greenstones, so called by early field geologists for their color. These were lavas evidently formed under water because they are structured in great blobs like those which form when modern lavas erupt and cool on the ocean floor. The shield lavas may have erupted when the earth was hotter than today. Their characteristic ore is iron.

Greenstones weave across the shield north of Lake Superior, ringing Hudson Bay on the south and east and reaching into Minnesota and beneath the plains to the Rockies. Another broad class of shield rock is sedimentary—limestones, sandstones, and shales—resting upon older granites. Around Lake Superior lie pockets of sedimentary rocks rich in copper, silver, and uranium. And in Wisconsin and Michigan just south of Lake Superior, some large diamonds have been found in the scramble of soil and gravel, probably deposited there by glacial ice from Precambrian rocks lying to the north. Intriguing deposits of diamond-associated minerals have been found near the tamarack swamps.

Some twenty thousand years ago, the great glacier that covered the North Woods with ice up to two miles thick began to melt. By six thousand years ago it had all but vanished from the continent.

The ice sheet was like a river of syrup, spreading slowly under great pressure to the south. It moved only inches a day, but nothing resisted it for long. Hills, even mountains, crumbled in its path. And then, upon reaching the Great Plains and as far south as the Ohio River, it began to break up. The bare rock of the Canadian Shield was left because the glaciers carried far to the south and west the soil cover it once possessed.

As millions of cubic miles of ice turned to water, rivers like the St. Lawrence and Mississippi were overwhelmed. It was during this time the great flood plains of rivers were created much as we know them today. The vast sprawling bottomlands of the Mississippi were actually the bottom of the river. It was a dramatic period and, in man's measurement of time, lasted thousands of generations. When the ice had receded, it left a barren landscape filled with potholes and lakes. The earth was sterile. But soon new life would begin. It would take thousands of years before the vast boreal forest would seed and thrive, but it would come. **37**

As the trees sprouted and grew, other plants formed an understory—bearberries, blueberries, and wild roses vied for space, each season laying down new deposits of mulch to decay during the winter; adding consistently to the soil-building process. Animals came too—types that have long since become extinct, but which now are replaced by black bear, musk oxen, mink, ermine, marten, muskrat, lynx, wolverine, beaver, and wolves. Moose and white-tailed deer roam much of the woodland. The musk ox is found only in the far Canadian north.

Nature's engineer, the beaver, began to work on the streams, damming them up into beaver ponds that again contributed to the smaller and more fragile forms of life. Hardly a North Woods stream today is without them. At one time they virtually disappeared, for their furs were much in demand. The Hudson Bay Company, the North West Company, and other lesser known ones vied hotly for their pelts during the early days. And from a population that once numbered in the millions, the beavers were reduced by trapping almost to the point of extinction. They became exceedingly scarce in Minnesota and Wisconsin. The beavers are now coming back, though in nothing like their original numbers.

Viewed from ground level, even a small segment of the North Woods looms an infinity of trees—somber, brooding, monotonous, yet overpowering in their mass. But when one studies the environment of this place, he is quick to realize that water is a force even more to be reckoned with in this wilderness. It is there in great abundance and variety. Minnesota on its license plates claims 10,000 lakes, Manitoba in Canada another 100,000. Neither claim seems exaggerated. In the 873,847-acre Boundary Waters Canoe Area alone there are some 2,500 lakes ten acres or larger in size. Many of the lakes feed the streams flowing from this country, keeping them supplied during even the driest months.

The Pigeon River of Minnesota is an unusual stream. For most of its length it peacefully wanders past reedy banks over a bed of mud; on occasion the water is only inches deep. At such places it is full of wildfowl, with ducks clattering, kingfishers rocketing into its calm surface in quest of dinner, or a great heron poking its long bill among the reeds. Then suddenly, the river's mood changes; it goes berserk on rapids or plunges abruptly over a precipice, where its placid brown water turns to roaring yellow foam. Below the point where the Grand Portage trail reaches it, the river becomes completely uncontrollable, erupting in a series of wild cascades through gloomy, echoing canyons.

The marks left by the glacier's passing are plentiful in the North Woods today, but one of the best examples is in the Granite River, which has numerous ledges that clearly show the planing and plucking action of the glaciers that passed this way; where the ice rode up on a rock ledge the surface is polished smooth, while at the other end, where the glacier froze to the ledge before moving onward, the rock is broken and split.

In areas throughout the North Woods are huge boulders, some as large as a house, called "erratics," left

5. This small plant—dicliptera—makes its home in a crack in the rocks along the Wolf River.

6. Long, late winter shadows are cast across the St. Croix flood plain in the Wisconsin woods.

7. A porcupine peeks through a crotch of a paperbark birch of Minnesota's Pigeon River.

5

7

6

behind when the glacier melted. They have been traced to the point of their origin, hundreds of miles north of where they now lie. Some of these can be found along the Wolf River as well as along the Pigeon.

A surprising variety of wildlife is found along many of the North Woods rivers during the warm weather months, some of it year-round. The Northern bald eagle, osprey, great blue heron, green heron, Swainson's hawk, upland plover, and red-tailed hawk mingle with mallards, blue-winged teal, common mergansers, canvasback ducks, and Canada geese. Of all the species of wildlife found here, the one most characteristic of the North Woods is the loon. I have often camped on a remote island on one of the rivers at night and listened to the forlorn warbling cry of the loon reverberating over the still water and through the groves of paperbark birch. Traveling in the North Woods gives me a sense of being in a different world altogether. As Florence Jaques wrote: "This country never knew a medieval time; it came straight from the primeval into today."

8

10

8. An early arrival during the spring migration from the south, this Canada goose looks for a suitable nesting site along the St. Croix River.

9. Sunset on the Wolf River of Wisconsin.

10. Wild mute swans often winter along the more remote stretches of Michigan's AuSable River.

3

RIVERS
OF
THE ROCKIES

Turning around, we can look through the cleft
through which we came
and see the river with towering walls beyond.
What a chamber for a resting-place is this!
Hewn from the solid rock, the
heavens for a ceiling, cascade fountains within.
—John Wesley Powell

*1. The Snake River, shown here
as it glides through Grand Teton National Park,
is appropriately named.*

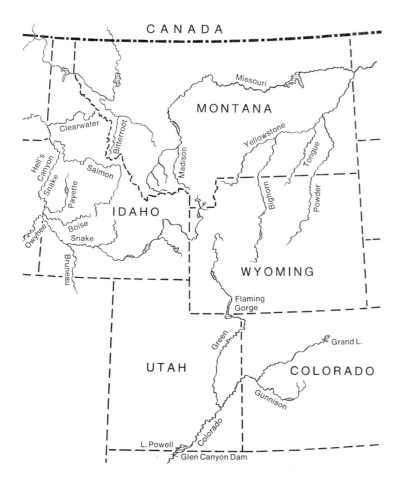

2. *The mountain rivers begin with little brooks such as this one, tributary of Idaho's Clearwater.*

"Incredible" is one of the few words that does justice to the Rockies, a land of magic sprawling across the geological backbone of America. With many peaks exceeding 14,000 feet above sea level, these mountains give geographical perspective to the rest of the nation, and the rivers blaze a frantic trail as they rush to escape the high country. Brawling, wild, and reckless, their spirit is complemented by the roar of angry whitewater, thundering over the falls and down the rapids. In their wake, they leave remarkable canyons as reminders of their violent past.

The rivers of the Rockies—as well as the terrain of which they are a part—linger in the mind's eye. Author Theodora Kroeber, who spent her childhood in the avalanche-wrecked mining hamlet of Telluride high in the San Juan Mountains of southwestern Colorado, remembers well: "In that thin dry air life moved at a pace of almost terrible intensity. There were no neutral moments—the galloping brevity of spring and summer, the long months of winter with the threat of tragedy always hanging near. Colors were high—the reds in the soil, the fall gold of the aspens, the indescribable sky. Riding in summer and tobogganing in winter were fast and dangerous; the heights of the mountains and the depths of the canyons were beyond the norm. . . . God was a pagan god, in the air, over the mountains, in the waterfalls."

Encompassing a geologically distinct area of some fifty ranges which extend from northern New Mexico to the Liard River country in northern British Columbia, the Rocky Mountains are part of a much larger mountain complex—a cordillera reaching ten thousand miles from Alaska to Patagonia that forms the backbone of two continents. We shall consider here only that portion within the United States, excluding Alaska.

The rivers of the Rockies drain some of the most remote country in the nation. Virtually no large cities are located along any of them. Many square miles through which they flow sustain not a single human life. Yet, by the same token, they have not escaped man's exploitation. The Colorado, for example, is perhaps the most used and abused river of the West. In the beginning, at Grand Lake in Colorado, its waters are pure enough to drink directly from the stream. As it snakes its way down to lower elevations, however, the Colorado is joined by tributaries whose waters are laden with the silt of flash floods. The Colorado then takes on a different character.

The early settlers who witnessed the Colorado had a phrase which aptly describes it to this day. They said its waters were "too thin to plow, too thick to drink." So during the first few hundred miles of its course, virtually all pollution of the Colorado is natural. It becomes a different story later as it reaches the fertile farmlands of lower California and Arizona.

The Colorado River country is vast and varied. In its canyons, changing life zones march up the sides with remarkable diversity—from thirsty creosote bushes at the lowest levels through stands of leafy hardwoods to cool forests of spruce and fir on the upper heights. At some places along the river, coyotes patrol sagebrush flats for rabbits, at others cougars prowl piney wood-

3. Water, of course, plays a great role in decay and in providing the ingredients needed to produce energy in the soil; here are the remnants of a great tree reduced virtually to humus.

4. Skeleton trunks of Douglas fir, spruce, and lodgepole pine are often found bleached by the sun in the wake of earthslides created by heavy rainfall in the Rockies.

3

4

5

6

5. *Great yellow pine grow in the Montana and Wyoming Rockies; drippings from their rain-soaked needles eventually may find their way into the Salmon or the Snake.*

6. *Wolves were once part of the Rockies environment; they have now virtually disappeared.*

7. The beaver, often referred to as the engineer of the riverways, constructs his home of sticks and mud, often right in the stream or along its edge.

8. Most Rocky Mountain rivers are as pristine as this upper portion of the Yellowstone, at least until they pass through our villages and cities.

7

8

lands for deer, and the skies are sometimes filled with hawks and occasional eagles scanning the cliffs of canyons for rock squirrels or, among the mesquite flatlands, an unsuspecting wily jackrabbit.

Much of the Colorado Plateau is characterized by horizontal surfaces etched into mesas and buttes, stone bridges and arches, ridges and canyons and colorful cliffs. The plateau was once uplifted by great forces deep within the earth, but the uplift was gentle and the layered sedimentary rocks were not greatly disturbed by the thrusting up. Over billions of years, the Colorado River has carved its way down through these layers, most spectacularly, of course, in the Grand Canyon.

There is simply no landscape on earth comparable to it. Extending some 277 miles in length, a mile deep and as much as eighteen miles wide in places, the Canyon is full of precipices, amphitheaters, buttes, and spires and nameless shapes in pink, green, and rust. The colors change in intensity and hue with each passing hour under the fierce Arizona sun.

Great nonconformities are found in the colorful canyon walls that tell of whole mountain ranges being totally worn away to leave a difference of 500 million years between the ages of two rock layers. Contained in the successive strata of rock is a record of evolving life that begins with evidence of one-celled plants dating back to the late Precambrian era. Hidden within canyon caves are the ruins of ancient civilizations.

The first white men to see the Grand Canyon were Spanish soldiers, members of an expedition led by Francisco Vasquez de Coronado, who reached the brink in the year 1540. In 1776, a Spanish missionary, Father Francisco Tomas Garces, climbed into a side canyon off the Colorado River to find a small tribe of Indians—the Havasupai—who treated him as a welcome visitor with five days of feasting. The Havasupai still live there along Havasupai Creek which empties a short distance downstream into the Colorado itself. Father Garces was the first man to refer consistently to the river as the Colorado, which means "red-colored" in Spanish and refers mainly to the brick-like hue of the silt-laden water.

During the next hundred years only a handful of white men—hunters, trappers, and, after the United States acquired the Southwest at the end of the war with Mexico, military surveyors—came near the Grand Canyon. It was not until shortly after the Civil War that the Colorado and its canyons were intensively explored. A one-armed Civil War veteran—geologist John Wesley Powell—mounted several expeditions down the Colorado by boat

It was on May 11, 1864, that Powell, with four boats and ten men, pushed off at Green River City, Wyoming, into the docile waters of the Green River to begin his first epoch-making adventure. Only three boats and six men would make it all the way to the Grand Wash Cliffs—more than one hundred days and 1,500 miles away. Three of them would die; the fourth, an adventurous Englishman, would leave the expedition at Uinta Creek. The six survivors would emerge from the unknown Colorado canyon country to conclude one of America's greatest exploration expeditions.

49

Powell himself foresaw little practical use for the waters of the Colorado, but by the turn of the century, the lower California desert country was being promoted as an imperial valley—a name that has stuck to this day. It was said to be ideally suited to farming with a 365-day-a-year growing season. Plenty of water was available, according to the promoters, from the nearby Colorado River. But what they didn't tell the newcomers was that the Colorado was totally unpredictable, that it was seasonal, overflowing its banks during the mountain snow runoff and dwindling down to a trickle during the dry summer and fall months.

In 1922 an agreement was signed giving each of the seven states laying claim to the Colorado exclusive use of 7.5 million acre-feet of water annually. Just eight years later, Congress enacted legislation providing for the construction of Hoover Dam, which would back up a tremendous reservoir of water on the lower Colorado, thus regulating the flow for agricultural convenience. It would be known as Lake Mead, located just outside Las Vegas, Nevada, in the driest portion of the Colorado Basin. Work began in 1931 on the concrete arch-gravity structure. Because of the immense amount of concrete to be poured (3½ million cubic yards), the dam was constructed in blocks through which ran steel tubing carrying water from the river to hasten the setting process. Had it not been for this cooling process allowing the concrete to settle more quickly, it would have taken more than one hundred years to dry.

In 1948, the upper basin states moved to insure their usage of the Colorado's water. They would build several dams. The major one was Glen Canyon, which many believe inundated a great natural splendor of the Colorado River second only to Grand Canyon. The Glen Canyon Dam was completed in 1964, backing up Lake Powell. Other dams were built at Flaming Gorge on the tributary Green River in Utah, at Blue Mesa and Morrow Point on the Gunnison in Colorado, and the Navajo Dam on the San Juan River in New Mexico. The Colorado and its tributaries would no longer run wild and free; it had now been harnessed for the will of man. Other dams would follow; the water would be diverted onto the land and into cities as far away as Los Angeles. And by the time the Colorado reaches Mexico today, it is diminished to a mere trickle.

Miles to the north and west from the origin of the Colorado begins another mighty Rocky Mountain river, the Snake, which wends 1,038 miles to join the Columbia in its quest for the sea. The Snake and its tributaries cover a wide variety of terrain ranging from the towering peaks of the Rockies and Grand Tetons in the upper reaches, lava plateaus in Idaho, to the deepest gorge on the North American continent at Hell's Canyon. At Shoshone Falls, the Snake plunges 212 feet over a 1,000-foot-wide horseshoe-shaped basalt rim in one of its most spectacular displays.

The Snake River is a naturalist's dream, and the least spoiled section along its route is that portion winding around and past the Grand Teton Mountains, a translucent green gliding swiftly over gravel or pausing in pools that reflect the forests and snow-draped peaks above. Osprey and bald eagle nest in tall trees overlook-

9. Here a tributary of the Colorado—Havasu Creek— seeks the larger stream on the Havasupai Indian Reservation.

10. The Clark's nutcracker.

11. The clearness of this water is partially due to the great filtering action of the stone bed of the stream.

9

10

11

12. The marmot, the watchman of
the high country, lives in rocky
burrows. These were photographed
along the Salmon River.

13. Ancient Indian hieroglyphics are
found on many of the stones and
boulders in remote areas of the
Snake River near Hells Canyon.

12

13

14

15

14. In parts of the Colorado
watershed, creosote bush and
mesquite struggle to survive on the
meager rainfall.

15. Throughout the more arid
mountain regions, as well as the
desert regions, one finds the horned
toad.

16

17

16. *Wind and water have been nature's greatest tools over eons of time, as evidenced by the great arches and red rock formations of Arches National Park along the Colorado watershed.*

17. *At Lee's Ferry, just downstream from Lake Powell, the Colorado begins to cut the canyon that ultimately will become the most spectacular of them all—Grand Canyon.*

18. *The actions of wind and water are plainly evident upon these sandstone formations around Lake Powell.*

19. *Dead Horse Point on the Green River shortly before it joins the mighty Colorado in southern Utah.*

18

19

20. *Magnificent waterfalls abound on some tributaries of the Colorado such as Havasu Falls near the bottom of the Grand Canyon. The water over the years has formed travertine limestone rims containing pools of the mineral-rich water.*

21. *Waterfalls, riffles, and rapids are much a part of the character of the magnificent Yellowstone River.*

22. Some say the noblest animal of the high country is the Wapita elk, shown here along the Yellowstone River.

23. The Wind River drainage in Wyoming, a spectacle of beauty.

23

22

24. *Elephanthead, so named because of a pendulous snout-like appendage from the flower. They are found throughout the Rockies, usually in damp places.*

25. *Multiflora, once used by the Indians to induce visions, grows along the Colorado.*

26. *Indian Paintbrush along the Lewis River in Yellowstone National Park.*

27. *The western sunflower is found along many of the Rocky Mountain streams.*

28. *The coneflower.*

60

29

29. Rabbitbrush, also called false goldenrod or goldenbush.

30. The snowy daisy.

30

ing the meadows where moose and elk graze and playful bears come to wallow in the summer sun. Beaver work diligently along this portion of the Snake, creating their own little private beaver ponds, trying in their own way to tame the river.

The upper Snake finds much of its way across a lava plain, a chaotic jumble of cinder cones, tunnels, tubes, and spattered vents that recall the lava beds of northern California. And like those, these are relatively new, being only about two thousand years old. Here the lava is less modified by erosion than at other places; very little soil has had time to accumulate upon it. Water from rainfall consequently sinks almost immediately into the lava to re-emerge elsewhere. Between Twin Falls and Bliss, Idaho, the Thousand Springs have a combined flow of nearly forty thousand gallons per second; eleven of the springs rank among the largest in the United States.

Generally, the river has not had enough time to dissect the lava plains very deeply, however, until it reaches Hell's Canyon. The general characteristic of the Snake River plains is one of utter flatness, built of lava that welled out quietly and profusely, flowing like a river of mud over the countryside.

At other places the lava has been worn down enough that it does not readily appear as lava at all. Sagebrush and cactus cover much of it, and a massive display of rubber rabbitbrush turns the landscape a brilliant yellow in late summer. Fernbush thrives here, too, as does bitterbrush, attractive to mule deer. Seeds of limber pine sustain the yellow-pine chipmunk, golden-mantled ground squirrel, and bushy-tailed woodrat. These and yellow-bellied marmots find refuge in lava holes and crevices from their archenemies—the red fox, coyote, and bobcat.

Although the Snake River has eight major tributary streams, none is more worthy of attention here than the Salmon, the legendary "River of No Return." Originating in the Sawtooth Valley and Lemhi Valley of central and eastern Idaho, this wild river (it has not a single dam on it) extends 425 miles. Rising at elevations above eight thousand feet, the Salmon drains fourteen thousand square miles during its cascading plunge to a level of only 905 feet at its mouth. A seventy-nine mile stretch between a point near West Fork and Riggins, Idaho, is generally known as the "River of No Return." Granite walls line many of the falls and rapids.

When Lewis and Clark reached the area in 1805, the Shoshone Indians told them the Tom-Agit-Pah could

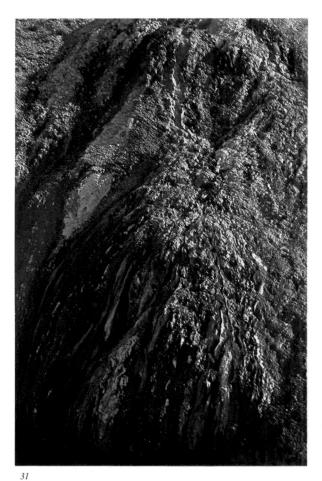

31. Hot water, rich in minerals, flows into the Firehole River in Yellowstone, leaving a rainbow of colors on the rock and soil.

32. Yellowstone's Minerva Terrace at Mammoth Hot Springs was formed by mineral deposits.

33. The early morning sun highlights clouds of steam escaping from the inner earth across the geyser fields of Yellowstone National Park.

34. Rivulets of iron-rust red waters escape from the geysers of Yellowstone and soon mingle with the cooler waters of the Firehole and Yellowstone rivers.

35. As the geyser water cools, mineral deposits and algae begin to build; life begins to form in the stream.

31

32

33

34

35

not be traveled in canoes. Cameahwait, brother of Sacajawea, the Indian maiden who guided the Lewis and Clark expedition, told them the river was so hemmed in by high rocks there was no possibility of traveling along the shore either.

Today most of the territory drained by the Salmon is public land, protected by the U.S. Forest Service. The Salmon starts in the Sawtooth National Forest, runs through the Challis National Forest, and marks a line between four others, embracing 7.8 million acres: the Salmon, Bitterroot, Nez Perce, and Payette National Forests. There are few signs of civilization along the course, save an occasional summer cabin.

Other tributaries of the Snake include the Clearwater, a highway for Lewis and Clark in 1805, which lies in northern Idaho's primitive wilderness; the Owyhee, which journeys north through the hot and barren southwestern Oregon desert; the Bruneau, a high desert stream discussed under Desert Rivers in this book; the Boise and the Payette rivers.

The headwaters for the Snake River system rise on the west side of the Continental Divide near Yellowstone National Park just a short distance from the beginnings of the Yellowstone River, which flows north and east to join the Missouri and ultimately the Mississippi drainage. In fact, there's a single small lake—Isa Lake—on the Continental Divide in Yellowstone which demonstrates well the division of waters. Its waters drain into the Snake, which flows northwest, and into the Yellowstone, flowing northeast.

The Yellowstone is a stream of trout and trumpeter swans, widgeon, white pelicans, buffalo, elk, mule deer, moose, and grizzly bear. No greater wildlife populations, nor more varied ones, exist along any river than along the Yellowstone, particularly in the Yellowstone National Park.

The Yellowstone has remained to this day a virtually wild river; no large dams check its seasonable flooding; there is no industry to speak of and very few towns along the way. But all this may soon change. New equipment and the energy crisis now makes mining the low-sulfur coal deposits in eastern Montana and northern Wyoming profitable. Strip-mining operations have already begun in Montana, and giant generating complexes are being built. The power companies now describe the area as "the Ruhr of the Northwest."

In order to make it possible for electricity generated in Montana to operate the air conditioners and pop-up toasters of Birmingham, Alabama, water as well as coal is required—millions of gallons of it. This water will have to come from containment dams on the Tongue, Big Horn, and Yellowstone, and the tragedy of the Colorado may be repeated.

At no other place in the nation are there more spirited rivers than those born in the Rockies. But the demands made upon these rivers by civilization and population grow greater year by year, and it is indeed sad that so much must be destroyed and sacrificed to man's domination of his planet. Where shall we be able to find wilderness a generation from now? How much of the magic of these western rivers and the lands through which they flow will have been engineered into oblivion for mere convenience?

4

TIDEWATER RIVERS

Earth's rivers form a huge,
constantly moving and changing web over the land.
Sculpturing the earth, channeling
their own courses and rechanneling them at will,
they plunge, leap, carom, or meander
lazily like live things.
—Peggy Wayburn/*The Edge of Life*

*1. Through the salt grass marshes the rivers
flow, sometimes to sea, sometimes pushed inland
by the relentless tides. Here is the vital breeding
ground of many marine creatures.*

2. *The estuary, the marsh, the river—all these combine into an ecological system unique to the low country. Both salt-water and fresh-water creatures and plants are found here, growing in an unusual mixture.*

The marsh awoke abruptly with a symphony of sound from the incessant call of green-winged teal, king rail, and mallards. It was early spring; the great sun suspended like a huge golden medallion over the misty grasslands, breathed new life upon this watery world of transition between the land and the sea. Warm breezes rippled the tough marsh grass, golden brown from the throes of winter.

To the west the marsh gradually gave way to the cypress swamps, their dark waters aswirl from spring rains shed in the Piedmont and the Appalachian Highlands where tidewater rivers are born. Below the fall line where the river breaks from the plateau to the low country, these streams, once reckless and rushing in their quest to escape the mountains, become docile meandering ribbons of silver. Their change in character is dramatic and sudden as they enter the lowlands, traditionally known as America's tidewater. Lying along the nation's southeast coast from Georgia to Virginia, the area that has come to be known as the Tidewater is a mixing bowl where saline waters of the ocean interact with the freshwater streams. Back and forth, twice a day as the tides rise and fall, the waters play upon each other; the end result is a brackish liquid that plays an integral role in the regeneration of many forms of life.

From the air, the tidewater appears as a network of interlacing ribbons along a scalloped coastline embroidered with marshlands. As it progresses toward the plateaus and mountains, the marsh turns to cypress forest and swamp, finally stepping up to the Piedmont Plateau, which today has been largely converted into an industrial and power-generating complex. Few rivers run free through it. But once they have reached the lowlands, most of their energy is spent and they are seldom harnessed.

The coastal tidewater area is broadest in the Carolinas and Georgia, but it is also a part of Virginia and includes such streams as the James, the lower Potomac, the Santee, Peedee, Edisto, Altamaha, and Savannah rivers.

While it is now a relatively small area of the continent, the tidewater at one time extended another two hundred miles to sea. During the last great Ice Age, the entire continental shelf was coastal plain—marshland. It drowned when glacial meltwater pouring back into the oceans raised the sea level.

Perhaps no single river better depicts the true tidewater stream than does the Savannah, born in the Piedmont by the confluence of four mountain rivers—the Chattooga and Tallulah, the Tugaloo and the Seneca. The Savannah then marches to the sea, its irregular path marking the boundary between South Carolina and Georgia for 314 miles. Along much of its course, the Savannah flows through plantation country; its banks lined with great live oak, hickory, elm, and magnolia. Downstream, these are replaced by such predominant trees as bald cypress and tupelo gum.

It was in this same area that great empires were built during the early days of this nation. First there was tobacco; then cotton became the economic base of the land. And still farther toward the sea were great rice plantations, but hurricanes in the late 1800s ended those ventures forever.

After rushing over Bull Sluice near Augusta, Georgia, the Savannah pours into the coastal plain. Here the banks are lined with rushes, reeds, and cane that lead back into giant cedar and cypress stands. A wild and nearly impenetrable jungle forms four to five miles deep from the river banks.

In few places has man penetrated this massive tangle of vines and trees; it is home to the cottonmouth moccasin, raccoon, great barred owl, the red-tailed kite, the pileated woodpecker. And in the dark, storied places of its innermost chambers is the breeding ground of the mosquito, a principal link in the food chain for a healthy wildlife population.

Wetlands such as Monkey John Swamp provided, as did much of the Savannah tidewater country, lumber for naval stores during the days of sailing ships. Yet its dense bottomlands appear to have grown unchecked for centuries, providing a unique sanctuary. A good part of the swamp is located within the Savannah National Refuge, with headquarters in Hardeeville, S.C.

Lying in both South Carolina and Georgia, the refuge's thirteen thousand acres are made up largely of the remains of old rice fields; the levees, foundations of slave quarters, old rice millsites, and small graveyards attest to the memory of these days back in the middle 1800s. For many years the industry flourished; it was a way of life here and no one thought it would ever end. But production overcame demand by the early 1870s. Hope had not been entirely lost, however, until 1893 when a disastrous hurricane swept up the coast from the Caribbean, wiping out the rice culture.

Once the Savannah River leaves the refuge, it passes the city of Savannah, then drifts through a delta land of sea islands, clad in squatty live oak and palmetto, that divide it into dark tidal channels. Oysters, shrimp, fiddler crab, and many other sea creatures live here. Beyond Tybee Island, an important shore bird sanctuary, the river at last issues forth into the Atlantic.

Not only is the Savannah an unusual tidewater river, it also has experienced a unique courtship with history. Discovered by the Spanish explorer Hernando de Soto in the spring of 1540, the first settlement—Savannah—was almost two hundred years later established as a refuge for English debtors by General James Olgethorpe. And just two years later, Oglethorpe built Fort Augusta upstream at the head of navigation.

After the demise of rice as the major cash crop of the lowlands, tobacco became a major consideration on the middle and upper portions of the river, but in 1793, Eli Whitney, while visiting Mulberry Grove plantation a few miles from Savannah, invented the cotton gin. Now it became profitable to process short-staple cotton. Flatboats, locally known as ''cotton boxes,'' drifted the muddy red river like hundreds of white clouds. Both Savannah and Augusta became great cotton trading centers. It was not until the area became diversified with other industry about the time of World War II and Savannah overshadowed Augusta as a major shipping and export center that all this changed. But the memories fostered by this lazy tidewater river remain;

3. Most of the day, the marsh along the tidewater river is seemingly void of life, but early in the morning the same scene will be vibrant with activity.

4. The Altamaha meanders across the coastal plain of Georgia, gathering its tributaries and casting its offering to the sea.

3

4

many of them are preserved along Savannah's thoroughfares.

Many of the tidewater rivers have strong historical connections. The James near Iron Gate, Virginia, formed by the Cowpasture and Jackson rivers, flows past the site of the first permanent English settlement, Jamestown. It was here on May 13, 1607, the *Susan Constant, Discovery,* and *Godspeed* were anchored and next day men and supplies were sent ashore to build the town. The first legislative assembly was held at Jamestown in 1619, but shortly before the turn of the next century, the capital was moved a short distance inland to Williamsburg.

The Potomac has one of the most extensive tidewater regions of all major rivers emptying into the Chesapeake Bay. Long before men navigated deep-draft, ocean-going vessels up the Potomac as far as the falls, white perch, herring, sturgeon, striped bass, and white shad entered the river each spring through its tidal outlet to spawn. That has not changed, but the numbers are only a fraction of what they were, mainly because of the overwhelming pollution in the stream.

Although diminished in its natural qualities by man's indifference to it, the Potomac is still an interesting

7

8

6

5. As the plants in a pothole grow and become thicker, more land is formed until ultimately the water is squeezed out and eliminated.

6. As you progress inland along the tidewater, you find interesting displays of reindeer moss on the higher elevations near the Piedmont.

7. The cardinal flower lends a flaming touch of color to the tidewater areas upstream from the marsh.

8. A common egret fishes along the Savannah River, intent upon catching its dinner from the small creatures swimming in the shallow water.

9. The downed marsh grass will rot and provide nutrients for the new shoots in the foreground.

10. (Overleaf) A dramatic lighting effect on the Altamaha, near the coast.

9

11

12

11. *A solitary common egret wings across the early morning marsh.*

12. *Willow primrose grows in the marsh area of the Savannah River.*

13. *A lone coot swims along the clogged waterways of the Savannah National Wildlife Refuge along the Savannah River.*

14. *Pickerel weed grows along the backwaters of the Savannah River. The tide surging back upstream has partly submerged the plants.*

13

14

river, even in its tidewater portion. Estuaries and secluded tributaries still are part of it—the Yeocomico, Nomini Bay, Smith Creek, the St. Mary's River, the Coan. Until World War II trading schooners still served innumerable hidden landings and villages on the Potomac, carrying lumber and produce to market. They're all gone now, those workhorse boats, their bones rotting in tidal marshes, but their ports of call still have much the same look and flavor.

The Potomac for many years was a major producer of oysters, of course, and it was not the illegal work of the oystermen that caused greatest damage. Instead, it was Hurricane Agnes. Oyster larvae require a delicate balance of salinity in order to insure a hatch and in 1972, Agnes roared up the Atlantic Coast and shot up the Chesapeake and Potomac to wreak devastation in many forms. The Potomac was backed up with salt water that spilled over into low-lying adjacent lands beyond Washington, and the oyster hatch has never been the same since.

Environmentalists say that the river is plagued not only with heavy doses of pollution but also with sediment coming down from the eroded and overcropped farmlands upstream, which is filling in the river from Maryland Point to Washington. Studies by the Maryland Department of Inland Fisheries show the spawning area for striped bass has been reduced rather drastically and is moving downstream. One official said that pollution and sedimentation are gradually overtaxing the estuary's recuperative powers. Soon, he said, it will be a sterile stream from Washington to the Chesapeake.

Perhaps the most pristine of all the tidewater rivers is the Altamaha flowing down through Georgia to enter the sea just north of Brunswick and Georgia's Golden Isles. It remains an area of marsh, swamp, and wetlands formed by the forces of nature countless years ago. It was this river which produced the habitat in which grew naturalist William Bartram's Franklinia Altamaha and some feel this rare flowering tree may still grow in some of the swamps there.

The thousands of acres of marshland along the Altamaha are important nurseries for shellfish as well as some finfish. Its swamps and wetlands are quiet places where dark clear water ripples and swirls and flows gently, where myriad wildflowers bloom and the rare prothonotary warbler sings, where otter, deer, mink, muskrat, and other animals thrive.

Shortly before the Altamaha loses itself in the sea, it flows around tiny Lewis Island, recently purchased by the state of Georgia to be preserved for posterity. On this tiny island remains the last virgin stand of bald cypress in the entire state, the only one found on the tidewater rivers. Many of the trees standing there on Lewis Island today were standing when Jamestown was built, when Oglethorpe founded Savannah, even when de Soto discovered the Savannah River and the tidewater lowlands.

The Tidewater, in many respects, is a timeless place, for its relationship with the sea is an infinite and continuing alchemy. It clearly reenacts a drama of life and death and rebirth staged in similar fashion long before man's appearance on earth.

5

ARCTIC
RIVERS

Like winds and sunsets,
wild things were taken for granted
until progress began to do away with them.
—Aldo Leopold

1. The Yukon River.

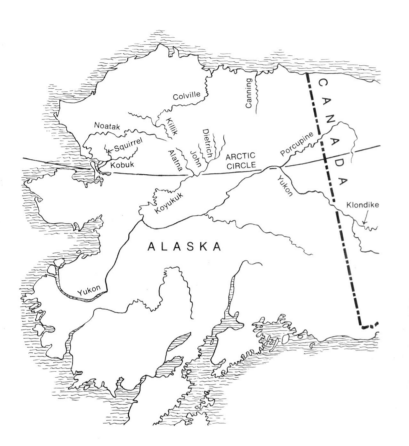

2. *Several Arctic streams are born in glaciers such as this one in the Brooks Range.*

Supreme Court Justice Oliver Wendell Holmes once said a river is more than an amenity. It is a treasure. That may well be true, but in the far north of our continent exist hundreds of rivers which are seldom, if ever, treasured simply because they are not generally known. These are rivers that flow into the Bering, Chukchi, and Beaufort seas from and through the forty-ninth state—Alaska. Many of them lie beyond the Arctic Circle.

The most publicized stream—mainly through the novels of Jack London—is the Yukon River. Counting its tributaries, the Yukon is the fifth largest river in America, beginning almost within sight of the Pacific Ocean and flowing more than two thousand miles north and west in its quest for the Bering Sea. Rising from a series of mountain lakes along the east flank of the coastal range in northwest British Columbia, the river drains some 330,000 square miles (only 60 percent of it in Alaska) of the most varied and scenic territory in this hemisphere.

The Yukon, while certainly an interesting and legendary stream, is hardly to be considered an Arctic river. Only a very short section of it sweeps beyond the Arctic Circle at a point near Fort Yukon north of Fairbanks. But there are many other true Arctic streams flowing through Alaska which offer an insight into a most fragile and unusual landscape.

Stretching only 450 miles—a short distance compared to many of the rivers in Alaska—the Noatak River rises in the residual glaciers of Mount Igikpak (elevation: 8,510 feet), highest peak in the Brooks Range, and dashes to the lowlands. Much of the upper portions of the land drained by the Noatak is tundra, but just before its midsection, the landscape changes to sparse stands of spruce, remnants of the northwesternmost range of the great boreal forest generally known as the North Woods. The trees are stunted, for there is little precipitation here—the average rainfall is only about ten inches, less than in some deserts.

In its midsection, the river grinds through its own Grand Canyon, a seventy-mile-long valley bordered by steep precipices, then cuts for six miles through the spectacular Noatak Canyon, a true river gorge with sheer cliffs on either side. Once below the canyon, the river finds itself in the midst of dense forest and again a broad valley—the Noatak Flats. It divides into several channels that braid in and out, weaving a remarkable pattern of ponds, sloughs, and shallow gravel and sandbars. Waterfowl, particularly whistling swans, during the summer months find this an ideal habitat for raising their young. Canada geese, snow geese, and ducks also cohabit this area from June until late September. They then leave ahead of the freeze to find warmer climes far down the coast in Oregon and California. Some even range east to join the eastern flyway and winter in the Carolinas.

Dr. William Sladen of Johns Hopkins University in Maryland, who began studying the area in 1971 in cooperation with the U.S. Fish & Wildlife Service, was able to trace some of the birds through a banding program. The swans were later sighted in Utah, Califor-

3. Immature Dall sheep cross an open area near the timber line in the Arctic high country.

4. The Alatna River, a tributary of the Koyukuk, which in turn joins the Yukon, meanders through territory unoccupied by man.

3

Alaska Field Office, Bureau of Outdoor Recreation

4

Alaska Field Office, Bureau of Outdoor Recreation

nia, and even in Maryland. Legislation is now pending in Congress to set aside the Noatak Valley, as part of a 7.6-million-acre area also including Squirrel River valley, to be a National Wildlife Range.

The Noatak is also a study in types of arctic habitat. Some five hundred species of vascular plants grow here, giving the Noatak a unique range of flora. Botanists say flora found here is as broad as that of the entire Alaskan Arctic Slope and larger than the flora of the whole Canadian arctic archipelago. Since it is close to the region where North America and Asia once were joined by a land bridge, it's felt the Noatak Valley is a prime location for studying a rich biota found in the arctic of both continents.

But practically every river in the Arctic is marred by caribou migrations—the Alatna, the Canning, the John, the Killik. The caribou, numbering in the thousands, make a greater impact upon the fragile tundra than any other creature save man. The herds flow over the land, consuming tons of vegetation a day. The sharp hooves cut trails not only into the soil but even into the rocks of mountain passes. The din of grunting animals and clicking hooves sounds far across the tundra, signaling all creatures that the moving tide approaches. Forever on the move, they emerge from the Brooks Range and trot onto the windswept barrens, appearing on one distant horizon and vanishing on the other.

Some of the herds winter in the Alaskan Range and migrate to the calving grounds on the North Slope during the summer. The cows to give birth come first, followed by barren cows and the bulls. But they actually range over many habitats—mountains, tundra, evergreen forests, ponds and lakes, bogs, at the edge of the sea.

Once the migration begins, nothing will deter it. When the caribou tide comes to the river, it moves through it, wading, swimming, always pushing ahead. Wolves forever haunt the herds, but they are not the greatest enemy. The mosquitoes here are so numerous that they can sap up to a gallon of blood from any living creature on the summer tundra within a few hours. While the caribou are protected by heavy fur, the mosquitoes attack the young on the nose and around the eyes, even inside the ears. And unless the mother caribou is around to help keep the mosquitoes away, the calf will die within a few hours.

Since the wet areas along the rivers normally harbor greater concentrations of mosquitoes than other areas, the caribou do not tarry along the streams. They come to drink, cross, and are soon on their way. If they can find a patch of snow to rest or spend the night, that is where they gather.

The predominant landscape of the Arctic, of course, is tundra, permanently frozen to depths of more than 2,000 feet. Covering some three million square miles, it is a most unusual landscape, for even though permanently frozen, some one to two feet near the surface thaws out by late May or early June, giving brilliant life to many types of lichens and plants. It seems as if all the flowers bloom on a single day, giving the tundra a sudden burst of brilliant color: poppies, mountain avens, lupines, rosebay, and heather. More than 1,500 **81** species grow in the Arctic and subarctic and they are remarkably adapted to such a harsh environment. Many of the plants spend the winter with their seeds in an advanced state of germination. Flowers freeze stiff during cold snaps, then thaw out to resume immediate growth, and the Plant Research Institute in Ottawa, Canada even discovered seeds of Arctic lupine frozen for more than ten thousand years...and yet they germinated and grew when exposed to the sun.

In winter, of course, the landscape turns to white and with blowing snow, the terrain is often undistinguishable from the sky. The entire atmosphere becomes a white-out, and nothing moves through it. The first snows come sometimes as early as late August or September, and by October and early November, all open water on the tundra is cast in ice for the long hard winter. Darkness comes, too, and lasts for days during January. Temperatures often drop into the fifty-below range and stay there for interminable periods. Only when the sun shows faintly above the horizon in February does it begin again to warm up. By the same token, during summer in the northern parts of the Arctic, the sun does not set for as long as fourteen days, but only drops low and circles above the horizon.

While most of the rivers in north or central Alaska have never been closely enough associated with man to possess unusual sociological history, the Yukon has a colorful one. Mainly it dates from the days of the early trappers who came into this country, often by way of the river, to seek their fortunes in furs. Then came the great gold rush—the Klondike and others along tributary streams. The Yukon became a way of life as steamers transported goods, equipment, and men to and from the gold fields to towns and villages. Gold has been found along several streams in Alaska, and placer mining as well as panning continues to this day. Occasionally one runs across an oldtimer who has never known anything else—gold has been his entire life. Never has he made it big, but always he has been able to eke out a good living from the river in gold nuggets.

Few sights in Alaska can compare with the view from the North Fork of the Koyukuk River, which flanks the area that wilderness proponent Bob Marshall aptly named the Gates of the Arctic. It may soon be a great national park in the central sector of the Brooks Range where impressive glaciated, gaunt, craggy pinnacles guard the edge of the continent across most of northern Alaska. Marshall so named the area because of two peaks dramatically flanking the river—Frigid Crags and Boreal Mountain. The park extends from a divide near the Dietrich River Valley west to the upper drainage of the Noatak and Kobuk rivers.

As one views this spellbinding landscape of the Gates of the Arctic, one senses that the real and lasting value of this land lies not in the gold found here, nor in the rich oil deposits under the North Slope, but instead in something far more lasting: the broad valleys, the subtle beauty of the tundra, the majesty of the mountains, the clear streams rushing toward the icy seas. The oil will be pumped out, utilized in the populated centers of the lower forty-eight, and nothing will be left. But the rivers and the landscape, we hope, will survive.

82

5 *Alaska Field Office, Bureau of Outdoor Recreation*

6

7

5. *Barren mountains loom above the Alatna River upstream from Tahahula Lake. Wildlife, including great brown bear, abounds in this area.*

6. *Marshlands sometimes extend for miles on either side of Alaskan rivers; this one is the John River.*

7. *A brown bear with a freshly caught salmon from the Noatak; a seagull patiently waits for any morsels that might be left behind.*

8. *(Overleaf) A mountain meadow and stream above the timber line in the Brooks Range.* (Starling Childs Photo)

9

10

11

9. A fresh forest fire burn along the Noatak River is revegetated with dense stands of fire weed; other species soon will follow.

10. Wildflowers grow profusely along many Arctic streams. This member of the saxifrage family is saxifraga oppositofolia.

11. Another brilliant touch to the Alaskan landscape is this shrubby cinquefoil.

12. Caribou grazing on the tundra.

6

RIVERS
OF
THE PACIFIC

Mountains are seen beyond, rising
in bewildering abundance, range beyond range...
and nowhere may you meet with more varied
and delightful surprises than in the byways and
recesses of this sublime wilderness.
—John Muir

*1. The Columbia, running down from the high
country of Canada through eastern Washington's
parched grasslands, is one of the most
hauntingly beautiful rivers of the Pacific Coast,
in spite of the many hydroelectric plants along its
route.*

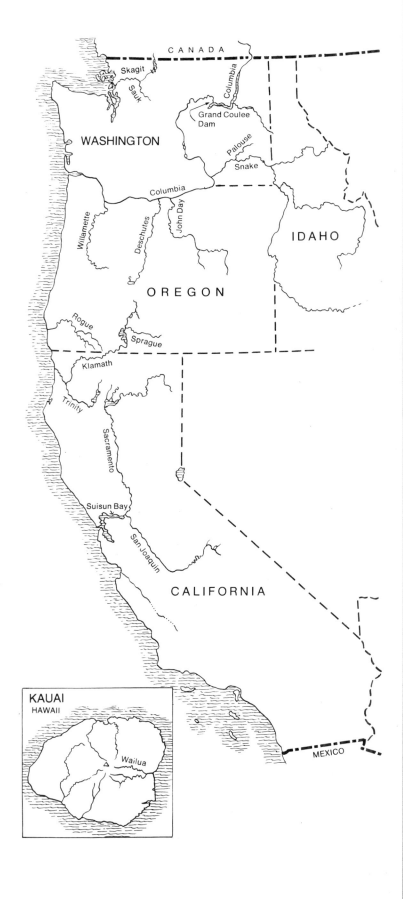

Along the Continental Divide in Yellowstone National Park is one of the most unusual small lakes in North America. From Isa Lake flow two small brooks—one on the east curves around and cuts its way across the Divide to flow ultimately into the Columbia River; the one on the west flows east to join the Yellowstone River and ultimately becomes a part of the Mississippi. Grass and water lilies growing on the lake dramatically demonstrate the direction of flow.

Although the main drive from the south entrance to Yellowstone actually crosses over the lake, few visitors notice it. But it tells a remarkable story, for this is the place—along the Continental Divide—where many of the rivers of the Pacific Coast begin. One can trace the course from the tiny rippling brooks along the periphery into the larger streams, small rivers to larger ones, one leading to another like a fine network of veins carrying back to the sea the lifeblood that sustains both it and the land.

The Pacific rivers are as diverse, however, as the land through which they flow. The Columbia is by far the largest and most complex, but it is also the most abused and used river on the continent. Other notable rivers emptying into the Pacific Ocean include the Sacramento and San Joaquin of California, the Skagit of Washington, the Rogue of Oregon, and a dozen relatives. They pick their way across arid lands, broad agricultural valleys, and dense rain forests. They cut spectacular gorges through the coastal mountains.

The Columbia River drains an area larger than France, dropping 2,650 feet in its 1,214-mile course from its source in the Canadian Rockies to the Pacific by way of Washington and Oregon. The Columbia and its tributaries generate almost three times as much electricity as all one hundred or more rivers of the Soviet Union's Volga system, ten times as much as the Colorado, and thirteen times as much as the Mississippi. Construction on the first great dam—the Grand Coulee—was begun during the era of Franklin D. Roosevelt's administration in the 1930s, and efforts continue even now to further harness the Columbia.

The dams, of course, have rendered the river more a series of lakes than anything else. Nonetheless, it still possesses a mystical beauty and charm that few rivers have. From Columbia Lake in British Columbia, the stream courses five hundred miles through a blue-forested alpine wilderness carpeted with wildflowers, densely populated with moose, bear, and bald eagles.

Crossing the border into Washington, the Columbia finds itself in the midst of rich agricultural lands—wheat fields roll to the horizon and beyond. Still there are few people; only small towns and villages border her banks. The Palouse River, one of the many tributaries, is located in that same type of remote rolling prairie country which turns various shades of brown most of the year for lack of water.

Onward the Columbia rolls, gathering tributaries from most of Idaho, Washington, and Oregon and parts of Montana, Wyoming, Utah, and Nevada via the Snake and Salmon. It finds its way through the Cascades where winter snows pile high and linger long, past lush forests of spruce and hemlock and pine, past

2. As the Columbia progresses westward to the sea, its environment changes several times from mountains to arid grasslands to rain forest.

3. Sunflowers, an important food for wildlife upon maturity, grow along many of the Pacific Coast rivers.

Tom Telfer

5

4. *Some of the Pacific rivers drain great forests of Douglas fir, lodgepole pine, yellow pine, and spruce. Heavy rainfalls in the Pacific Northwest provide conditions for dense growth.*

5. *The Wailua River on the Hawaiian island of Kauai cascades over a volcanic formation.*

6

6. *Cliff swallows nest in burrows along ancient cliffs left by the Columbia River.*

7. *Backwaters along the Columbia create a lakelike shoreline that swells and meanders, creating marsh oases in an arid mountainous land.*

8. *Goatsbeard, prized as a "honey" plant, grows along many of the Pacific Coast rivers.*

9. *Flocks of pigeons live in the cliffs at Palouse Falls in eastern Washington.*

10. *(Overleaf) The Columbia skirts the mountains, seeking its way to the Pacific.*

7

8

9

the snow-capped volcanic cones of Mt. St. Helens, Mt. Adams, and Mount Hood.

The shortest route to the sea is seldom the one taken by a river, and the Columbia is no exception. It flows northwest for the first 218 miles, then south for 280 miles, then west and then south again in a sweeping curve called the Big Bend. Many deep channels have been cut by the river, leaving a series of coulees or dry canyons. The largest is Grand Coulee, of course. Just below the mouth of the Snake, the Columbia cuts across the Cascade Range through the scenic Columbia River Gorge forming the boundary between Washington and Oregon. At Vancouver, Washington, it again turns north for fifty miles, then west for the final fifty-five-mile run to the Pacific. Tides affect it as far as 145 miles from its mouth.

More than a thousand miles southwest of the Columbia, climate and volcanic activity have created another, very different type of river. The Wailua and other rivers in Hawaii exist in areas that rather recently (in geologic terms) were active. The Wailua, located on the island of Kauai, commonly known as the Garden Isle of the Hawaii cluster, flows through an interminable jungle, part of which is inundated with the highest rainfall in the world. On Mt. Waialeale fall more than 450 inches of rain annually, sometimes more than forty inches in a single twenty-four-hour period. Since Mt. Waialeale is the single summit of Kauai, rivers—including the Wailua—fan out in every direction from the mountain.

Because of these heavy downpours, the rivers fluctuate dramatically, and only the heavy, compact soil, reinforced with root systems of the dense vegetation, keeps the high waters from flushing away the banks.

None of the other Pacific mainland rivers are so blessed with rainfall; some of the area drained by the Columbia and Sacramento gets no more than ten inches a year. And, of course, that's another reason these rivers have been so impounded; they store water for use in irrigation and, in some cases, for human consumption.

Up north in Washington, the Skagit has been less affected by man, but neither does it flow free. Like the Columbia, it also begins in British Columbia and, after crossing into the United States, flows through a series of reservoirs—Seattle, Ross, Diablo, and Gorge—created by the Seattle Department of Lighting. From the company town of Newhalem, the Skagit flows through a deep canyon to its confluence with the Cascade River. The river valley then becomes progressively wider, eventually to form a broad bottomland.

Where the Skagit is joined by the Sauk River is a traditional wintering ground for the American bald eagle. Ornithologists have counted as many as one hundred in a single day along a thirty-seven-mile stretch of the stream. They come there to fish for vast populations of steelhead in the river. The river and its tributaries support eight species of anadromous fish—that is, fish that live portions of their life in the sea—five species of salmon, steelhead, sea-run cutthroat trout, and Dolly Varden.

The salmon run up the Columbia is one of the most impressive natural spectacles anywhere. They come by

11. *During the waning hours of the day, the sprawling Columbia reflects an August sunset.*

12. *The Sacramento drains an area that once experienced great volcanic activity. These volcanic boulders were tossed across a California hillside north of the capital city in recent geologic times.*

13. *Big Springs at Mount Shasta contributes much of the water at the beginning of the Sacramento River flowing down from northern California.*

14. *As the Sacramento joins with the San Joaquin east of San Francisco, it creates marshlands and swampy areas reminiscent of a southern river.*

13

14

the millions, making their way past the great dams via fish ladders, bent upon reaching the upstream spawning grounds. The Yakima and Clatsop Indians regarded the salmon as supernatural beings and propitiated them with suitable rites and prayers. After spending their first one to two years in the river, the young salmon head back to the Pacific, where they wander for one to two more years, sometimes traveling as far as Japan and up to the Bering Sea. Eventually they return to the stream where they were born to spawn and, after doing so, die.

The Sacramento, which runs south from a huge spring in the shadow of permanently snow-covered Mt. Shasta in northern California, is a quieter type of Pacific river, and the salmon do not breed here. It extends for some 370 miles, and joins the San Joaquin to form the fertile California delta before flowing into the Suisun Bay fifty miles west. The apparent calm of the Sacramento can be deceptive, however, for it carries an average annual runoff of 22,390,000 acre-feet, more water than is carried by the Colorado.

It was on a tributary of the Sacramento that one of America's most significant historical events occurred back on January 24, 1848. Gold was discovered by James W. Marshall while working at John Sutter's sawmill at Coloma on the South Fork of the American River just thirty-five miles northeast of Sacramento. When Marshall reported his find to his boss, Sutter tried to suppress the news, but it soon got out anyway, and the California gold rush was on. Two years later, the state's population had gained another 100,000 people, most of them looking for gold.

The gold was mined and panned, and within a few years the operation lived only in history books. But the Sacramento River had established itself as a commercial waterway during that era. There is less traffic on the river today, but it does provide the water for much irrigation down the valley. And it also is, through a string of national wildlife refuges along it, a wintering place for much of the waterfowl that comes down the Pacific flyway. Snow geese, Canada, and the Ross's goose make the Sacramento Valley a destination.

One of the most awesome Pacific Coast rivers is the Klamath, which begins as the Link River in south central Oregon. The 263-mile stream of the Klamath provides a grandeur few rivers can match. Dropping one hundred to two hundred feet per mile, it moves southwesterly across the border into California and then is joined by its principal tributary, the Trinity River. The upper Klamath flows through an isolated wilderness of tree-choked gorges. An incredible number of salmon, sturgeon, trout, and steelhead are found here, while California quail rustle through the understory. Seagulls and eagles share perches on the rocks and in the trees along its path.

So the rivers flowing into the Pacific from the West Coast and from America's fiftieth state are indeed varied and colorful. All are undergoing change, most of it for the worse. But environmental groups and an increasing number of government agencies are striving to keep them as they are, to preserve them so that something of their original character will be left for generations to follow.

7

DESERT RIVERS

Nearly every striking feature
of this special world...goes back ultimately
to the grand fact of dryness—the dryness
of the ground, of the air,
of the whole sum-total.
—Joseph Wood Krutch/*The Voice of the Desert*

*1. The desert appears void of water, but there are
streams which drain the waters from the heart of
it. This is the Arizona-Sonora Desert of Arizona
and Mexico.*

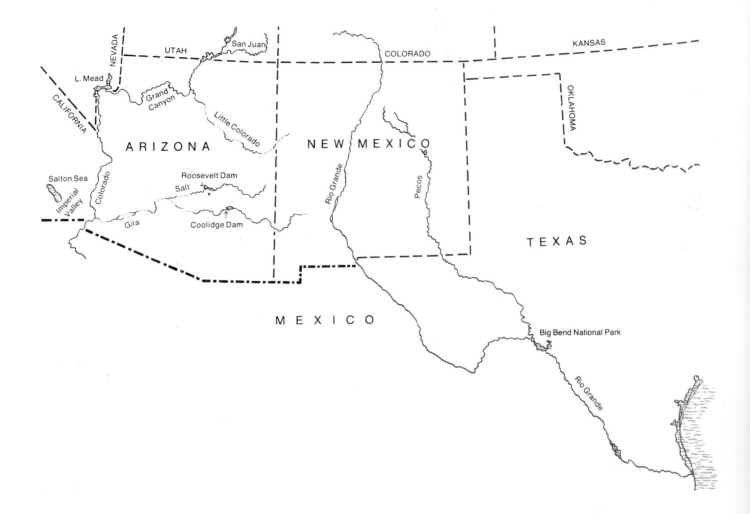

The desert is one of the world's most remarkable landscapes, and the desert river is just as unique. As it curls across the thirsty land in its search for the sea, loaded with silt and covered with dust, the desert river is often hardly a river at all; in many places it is reduced to a mere trickle by a scorching sun and the demands of the land through which it flows.

The word "desert" comes from a Latin adjective meaning "abandoned." To many of the early travelers in the west and southwestern United States, the very mention of deserts conjured up visions of desolate stretches of sand, dry lakes and streams, distant buttes shimmering in hundred-degree heat. But what bothered them most of all was the lack of water. And water, indeed, is a rare commodity in the desert.

Few desert rivers are born in the desert itself. The Rio Grande, for example, begins in the San Juan Mountains of southern Colorado, and for the first eighty miles it is largely a mountain stream, wild and beautiful. But then it soon reaches the arid lands of New Mexico, slices its way through dusty canyons, and ultimately becomes the dividing line between the United States and Mexico. For most of its 1,800 miles, the Rio Grande flows through arid or desert lands. Along its lower reaches, where it has created a fertile alluvial plain, the nation's finest vegetable farms are located, tapping the waters of the river to give the desert life before it meanders into the Gulf of Mexico.

Draining an area of 240,000 square miles, its tributaries extending like fingers into both the United States and Mexico, the Rio Grande is sometimes hard put to gather enough water to get to the sea. At other times of year, when the skies erupt and spill their burden upon the thirsty desert, the Rio Grande becomes a raging torrent tumbling boulders, tearing away embankments, overwhelming any obstacle in its path. The flash flood is much a part of the character of any desert river: the Rio Grande, the Gila, the Salt, the San Juan, and the Little Colorado, to name a few. When it rains in the desert, there is no humus in the soil to soak up the drops of water and detain them for another day, so the water runs into branches or dry washes which themselves become sudden-born rivers. Soon a flash flood is underway. For a few minutes or a few hours, the desert sparkles with moisture. But it is soon gone and by the next day there is little trace left of even a heavy rainfall.

Most of the desert regions get less than ten inches of rainfall annually. Sometimes, it may come in one or two downpours, the next rain another year away. But this one storm usually has great impact upon the desert and upon the desert river, for which each flash flood, something about the stream is changed. It may be the

3

2. *The Rio Grande is one of the most scenic desert rivers, partic- ularly where it flows through great canyons in Big Bend National Park, Texas. The right wall is in Mexico.*

3. *Willows crowd the bank, affording it some protection against the desert river. Snakes, roadrunners, and a multitude of desert wildlife take refuge in these damp places along the desert streams.*

4. *Crownbeard or butter daisy is one of the colorful little flowering plants found in the arid country along the Rio Grande.*

5. *The desert bighorn sheep is a shy creature seldom seen by man. It thrives in rocky areas in the desert.*

4

5

entire channel in some places; the embankments, parched to flakiness, are readily carried downstream by turbulent floodwaters.

No other type of river in America has greater soil removal capabilities than the desert river and no river is less predictable. With each high water period, it is tearing down, carrying away, building up in another location. The land is consistently on the move in the desert, thanks to the combined action of wind and water. But the flash flood plays the major role.

Take, for example, the San Juan River, which drains some of the Navajo country of northern Arizona including Monument Valley. Each year this small stream carries more than thirty-four-million tons of sand, mud, and gravel away. During one extraordinary day of flood on October 14, 1941, the river transported an estimated twelve-million tons of sediment past the village of Mexican Hat, Utah, where it was being monitored. The annual load would fill enough average-size dump trucks to stretch, one behind the other, around the earth at the equator eight times. By comparison, the Mississippi River carries only 340,000 tons of sediment past St. Paul, Minnesota, annually.

The sediment and silt are not the only movements made by the river. It transports a huge but unmeasurable bed load as well—boulders, cobbles, and pebbles pushed along the stream bottom by the current. During high water on the San Juan, there is a constant clunk as the boulders strike each other rolling downriver, thirty feet below the surface. The same is true of the Rio Grande as it funnels its way through Santa Elena and Mariscal canyons.

During these flood times, the rivers of the desert become something between liquid and solid, almost like a wet avalanche. Normally the sediment load may be only one or two percent, but during flood it may reach as high as 75 to 80 percent. The watery silt of the bottom and the silty water of the current above it form a single viscous substance in continous flux. On the river bottom, underwater sand and silt dunes are constantly building, being torn down, rebuilding.

While flash floods may occur at any season of the year, they are most common during the springtime. The storm clouds gather suddenly and, accompanied by the rattle of thunder and a tumultuous display of lightning, sweep angrily across the desert landscape. The clouds burst, the raindrops explode upon the parched earth in a crescendo of violence, and soon the sparse desert plants may be standing in a sheet of water. The dry washes marked only by the last rain, perhaps months ago, quickly fill up. Desert rivers have been known to rise ten feet or more an hour, then retreat to a trickle in the next hour as the waters sink into the porous gravel of the stream bed.

The drama in the skies is shortlived and the storm is often localized. In fact, most flash floods are also accompanied by colorful rainbows, for the sun is never far away, even during the heaviest downpour.

During the day the desert is largely devoid of wildlife—or so it seems. But immediately following the flash flood, the desert comes alive. Snakes, lizards, and small rodents run helter-skelter, routed from their burrows by the flood. As soon as the rain stops, other

107

6. The gila woodpecker, found virtually no other place than in the extreme southwest desert, lives on insects procured mostly from cactus.

7. Many desert streams flow only after a flash flood, but over the years they have etched their way into the heart of the hard desert rock.

8. Displaying distinctive yellow spots and the black neck bands that inspire its name, the collared lizard feeds mostly on young snakes, small birds, and other lizards.

9. The raccoon also is found in the desert, holing up in the rocks by day and prowling at night.

10. This could be the makings of a great canyon, given eons of time for the wind and water to carve it ever deeper and wider.

11. (Overleaf) Portions of the Colorado River flow through great desert. Here it provides the waters for Lake Powell shown under a full-moon desert sky in Arizona's Navaho country.

6

7

8

9

10

12. *Young desert bobcats doze through the heat of the day in a rocky crevice.*

13. *The coatimundi, known locally to Arizonans as the chulu, is a tropical relative of the raccoon but considerably larger. An omnivorous feeder, it can easily scale trees and often is found snoozing in them.*

13

12

14

15

14. *The cholla cactus, also known as the teddy bear.*

15. *The barrel cactus has a fish-hook type thorn but displays colorful blossoms in August and September.*

16. *In the Arizona-Sonora Desert is found the saguaro cactus, which grows to more than 30 feet. Owls and other creatures live in burrows within them, opened by the gila woodpecker.*

17. *The ocotillo shrub is found in many desert regions including the Arizona-Sonora and the Mojave.*

18. *One of the most common cacti—the prickly pear.*

19. *The chain fruit cholla.*

20. *(Overleaf) The Chisos Mountains of Texas' Big Bend country; to the south of them runs the muddy Rio Grande.*

17

18

19

16

animals and a wide variety of birds begin to move about. The coyote, the bobcat, the hawk, and the eagle soon are out searching for prey. But the smaller creatures are bent upon survival. The rattlesnake may become a refugee alongside its bitter enemy, the roadrunner, both seeking higher ground, each oblivious of the other. So too the killer wasp and the hairy tarantula.

Then as suddenly as it came, the flash flood is gone, disappearing downstream. The hot sun helps to evaporate some of the water quickly, and the remainder is on its way to the sea, roaring through the canyons, dissipating into a sheet of water spreading over the flatlands. The waters give and take away wherever they go; they also alter the streambed. In the Rio Grande, the high waters create bancos, or islands. Sometimes even secondary bancos—an island sliced off from another island—are created along the Mexican-U.S. border. Along the lower Rio Grande, fertile alluvial bottomlands have become a patchwork of bancos and a maze of abandoned riverbeds.

Upon several occasions the Rio Grande has created international disputes over the boundary line between Mexico and the United States. It began with the Treaty of Guadalupe-Hidalgo in 1848 ending the Mexican War, which began just two years earlier. In that treaty, some 1,300 miles of the Rio Grande was designated as the boundary between the two countries, but little did either country realize at that time the problems the river would create.

Between 1856 and 1970 diplomats and engineers worked at applying an old principle that a boundary moves with any slow methodical process of erosion of one streambank and accretion to the other, but that if a new course is suddenly cut by the river, the boundary stays in the abandoned bed. The International Boundary Commission, established by treaty with Mexico in 1889, classified changes and by the time of the Mexican Revolution had settled more than one hundred cases.

Floodways and levees have recently been built to stabilize the channel of the Rio Grande from El Paso to Fort Quitman, reducing 155 miles of unchecked meander to eighty-eight miles of broad bends. And in the El Paso area, the river was moved northward, given a new curve, and firmly fixed in place in a concrete-lined channel.

Much of the Rio Grande remains wild and untamed. In the 700,000-acre Big Bend National Park the river flows through steep canyons and alluvial desertlands, just as it did several centuries ago. There are green pockets of cottonwood and willow along the river's edge, but the dominant contours are of arid, sweeping mesa and rolling mountain land.

It is in these areas along the Rio Grande that one finds greater concentrations of wildlife in the desert. Naturally they are attracted by water, and rabbits, roadrunners, various kinds of snakes, black vultures, coyotes, javalina, bobcat, and mountain lion range in close proximity to water supplies.

Perhaps the Rio Grande is most colorful in Santa Elena Canyon, a ten-mile stretch of sheer rock walls some 1,500 feet high. Buzzards, hawks, and eagles soar through the canyon, riding the thermals that play

21

along the reddish-yellow walls. Downstream is the Mariscal Canyon and, later, the Boquillas Canyon. In between are lowland areas of willows which rattlesnakes and roadrunners each claim as their domain.

Along the Salt and Gila rivers which bisect portions of the Arizona-Sonora Desert in Arizona, archeologists have found evidence of prehistoric attempts to conquer the desert. From about 300 B.C. to 1400 A.D., a culture referred to as the River Hohokam inhabited these valleys. The people were agricultural and apparently depended upon the natural flooding of the rivers to water their corn, beans, squash, and cotton.

Around 700 A.D. the Indians began irrigating crops through an elaborate system of canals, but by 1400 the river people had mysteriously disappeared. Theories point to partial or total destruction of their canals from excessive rainfall and a drop in crop productivity from too much salt in the soil. Others believe drought, enemies, or pestilence may have forced them away. The Gila cliff dwellings are still located in the Tonto National Monument; some canals were in existence until 1911 when Roosevelt Dam was built and they became inundated by the impounded lake. There still are some to be seen at Pueblo Grande in Phoenix.

Even though the desert river has been harnessed, its waters stolen away for irrigation, its channels changed or fixed, it remains a most unusual member of the family of American Rivers. It is genetically and ecologically different from any other stream to be found on earth.

21. *Between flash floods, plant life emerges from the dry desert stream bed and flourishes on underground moisture until another flood comes and washes it away.*

22. *After the flood has passed by, the hot sun bakes the stream bed, causing it to crack and blister.*

23. *On rare occasions, downpours inundate the desert. A 30-minute rainfall turned this stretch of desert between Tucson and Phoenix into a great lake stretching beyond the horizon.*

24. *Suddenly, as though by prearranged signal, the dry desert stream becomes a raging torrent, sweeping away everything in its path.*

25. *Sometimes only an hour later, the onslaught has passed and the sediment begins to clear from the remaining trickle of water; tomorrow this stream likely will be dry again.*

8

PRAIRIE RIVERS

An' the prairie an' the butte-tops an' the
long winds, when they blow,
Is like the things what Adam knew
on his birthday, long ago.
— Anonymous

*1. Many of the prairie rivers run virtually level
with the surface of the earth, as illustrated by
this section of the Platte.*

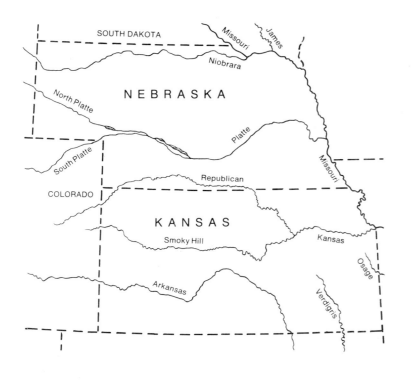

2. Prairies and buttes intermingle as the flat grasslands begin to merge with the mountains in western Nebraska. The Platte river, along which ran old wagon trails, flows nearby.

122

It was spring along the Verdigris River in what today is eastern Kansas. A light breeze made gentle waves in the tall prairie switchgrass and bluestem, and among the towering cottonwoods along the Verdigris it set the leaves rustling with the sound of pattering rain. A small group of Osage Indians, gaunt and tired from the long, harsh winter, worked leisurely setting up their summer camp along the river bank. Then there came another sound strange to the prairie country. At first it was a barely audible buzz. Then it grew louder as a small dark cloud appeared upon the horizon. As the cloud drew near, some of the Indians ran for cover; others stood mesmerized by the sight and sound until it had passed them by.

For the first time, the Osage had seen a swarm of honeybees. For them—and for the prairie—it was a bad omen. For they knew that not far behind would be the white settler. The Osage had heard of the honeybee. The Indians called them white man's flies. Word had been passed for months from the tribes to the east, filtering along the Indian grapevine to the Osage, the Sioux, the Paiute. The honeybee had swarmed across the broad Mississippi River around the turn of the nineteenth century and for the next several years these insects, introduced to the New World by the early colonists, continued to move westward. Progressing forty miles or so each year, they concentrated along the rivers of the prairies, for this is where the great trees grow that could be used as a hive to store honey.

The prairie was ideal for the honeybee. Here they could harvest pollen from never-ending horizons of wildflowers and various clovers. The rivers afforded them excellent free-flowing waters filtered down cold and clear from the Rockies and there was an abundance of great trees—mostly cottonwoods. The warm season was long. As the honeybee thrived, so did the settler who brought with him not only the honeybee but a desire to conquer the prairie and convert the land to his own use. The westward movement marked the end of the great virgin prairie and grasslands; only isolated pockets of it remain today.

As the endless prairies were altered by man, so were its rivers. Only in intermittent segments do they remain free-flowing and seemingly untouched, but those segments provide an interesting study of a stream that lies shallow in the earth, sometimes choking itself with sandbars, fingering its course along an uncertain path toward the Gulf of Mexico. Most of the prairie rivers find their sources in the Rockies, but their character is more influenced by the rolling hills and flatlands of the prairie. The Osage, the Platte, the Kansas, the Verdigris, the Niobrara; all of these ultimately rendezvous with another stream. Most of them empty into the muddy Missouri.

Once the prairies extended westward from Pennsylvania to the Rockies, from Texas into Canada, a billowing sea of grasses dotted with deep marshes, vegetation-rimmed sloughs, and abundant ponds. It was a place that provided range for a variety of wild creatures. The endless horizons were often black with a moving sea of bison; the spring and fall skies darkened with the annual migration of birds. This was the fabric **123**

John Ebeling

3

4

5

3. *Along the quiet pools of the Platte River are found colorful wood duck such as this male. A female and perhaps a nest will be nearby.*

4. *Spurge, more commonly known as snow on the mountain, grows along the Nebraska portion of the Platte river.*

5. *The Niobrara River, wending its way through the Fort Niobrara National Wildlife Refuge, has been little altered by man.*

6. *Mule deer graze much of the prairie river country. These live along the Niobrara River.*

6

7. In western Nebraska, the true West begins, marked by ancient cliffs and buttes created by wind and water.

8. One of the few Texas longhorn cattle surviving in North America, part of a herd on the Fort Niobrara National Wildlife Refuge of northern Nebraska.

of life for the prairie, the beauty of this place a century or more ago.

Today, the prairie country is generally said to begin in the Ozark foothills of Oklahoma and southeastern Kansas, extending northward through Nebraska's sandhills and the Dakotas into Canada. It is bordered on the east by the pin and scrub oak forests of Missouri, the corn and soybean fields of Iowa, and on the west by the Rockies and the arid desert country of eastern Wyoming and Montana. The most legitimate tract of tall grass prairie still in existence is Kansas's Flint Hills, south of Emporia and just west of the Verdigris. From vistas here, the prairie stretches beyond the horizon. The Santa Fe Trail once came this way, a narrow roadway parting this sea for the westward trek of prairie schooners. Tomorrow—or twenty years hence—this same area might well become the nucleus for a new national park to preserve some of this wonderful landscape.

The Osage River, running along the northern border of the Ozarks in Kansas, usually is heavily laden with mud and silt, but because of that, it has built numerous bars of mud, gravel, and sand. These gravel bars consti-

8

7

9. *The names and dates of early travelers are carved in the soft rock along the Platte.*

10. *The prickly poppy.*

11. *Pheasant are one of the finest game birds of the prairie river country...and one of the most colorful.*

12. *A tiny sundrop ekes out its existence on a barren rock along the western Platte River.*

13. *(Overleaf) Canada geese, many species of ducks, and the lesser sandhill crane are attracted to the Platte River valley during their migration.*

tute one of the few remaining spawning grounds of the paddlefish. One of the oddest looking creatures on earth, the paddlefish is a descendant of a 100-million-year-old family of fresh-water fishes that used to swim thick in the great rivers of America, particularly the Mississippi. It has a snout like a swordfish and gills equipped with comblike filaments, like the baleen in whales, with which it captures plankton. The internal skeleton of the paddlefish consists mainly of cartilage, like the shark's, and its skin is smooth like that of a catfish. Adults weigh from forty to fifty pounds each; one monster caught a few years ago was 163 pounds. Their gun-metal gray bodies sometimes reach six feet in length.

The Osage is identified with the paddlefish, but the Platte is associated with another creature which dates back into prehistory, virtually without evolutionary change. It's the lesser sandhill crane, and thousands of them come to the Platte in late winter or early spring. It's a rendezvous on the route north from the wintering grounds in Texas, along the Gulf Coast, and in Mexico. Here they rest, dance, feed upon the surrounding farmlands, and choose a mate.

All winter the Platte is quiet, much of it flowing gently under a window of ice. Then suddenly on a February morning, that silence is broken by the incomparable and unmistakable bugling call—Karoo, Karoo—as dawn breaks over the land. The great birds, standing four feet tall, are back. They roost on shoals and inlets, and sometimes cast a gauze of shadows across the shallow Platte. By mid-March, some 200,000 of them have gathered here, pausing on their annual migration north; some fly six hundred miles nonstop. The red-crowned, plumed sandhills feed, court, and loaf, marshaling in early April for the final flight to their nesting grounds in Canada and Alaska.

The Platte is a remarkable stream. Washington Irving once said: "The Platte would be quite a river if you could stand it on edge." It is often described as the river a mile wide and an inch deep, and in many places this is indeed an apt description. During spring floods, it can be a mile-wide torrent of destruction, gulping farms and bridges. Usually, though, it is a rambling series of streamlets flowing erratically over great sand and gravel fans that are, in part, the remnants of a mightier Ice Age stream bed. Quicksands and shifting islands haunt its waters. Over it the prairie sun beats mercilessly throughout the summer—from April until October. This transparent ripple throughout its history has wandered and meandered as it pleased through the Nebraska landscape, finding little resistance to erratic changes in its course.

Cutting toward the sunset as it did, the Platte River was like a compass to those traveling west. Its valley was a flat, easy corridor to the gold fields and the never-never land of farms and orchards in California and the Pacific Northwest. It provided water for the wagon trains and timber for wood, shade, and repairs. But there were disadvantages too —the buffalo trails.

Usually running perpendicular to the river's course and to the wagon train going west, the eroded ruts resulted in broken axles and mired wagons. Herds

14

15

14. *The buffalo (American bison) has all but disappeared, but a few small herds may still be found on the prairies and in the Black Hills of South Dakota. Here a great bull, weighing more than a ton, grazes along the Niobrara River.*

15. *An American bison cow and calf.*

16. *A herd of bison browse the rich grasslands of the Nebraska prairie.*

16

numbered not in the hundreds nor even in the thousands but in the tens of thousands, and a wagon train might travel through a congregation of the beasts for an entire day before passing them by. It was a spectacular sight, but a grueling experience little appreciated by road-weary immigrants.

Wolves, too, took the travelers' imagination and attention with their early morning howling that sent shivers up and down the spine. And each morning the men took tally to see how much livestock had been downed by these marauders during the night.

Today the wildlife of the river has changed, of course. The bison are all gone, but there are still bald and golden eagles which roost among the cottonwoods. Thousands of migrating mallards, ruddies, and pintails pass this way. Canada and snow geese stop here too, sometimes wintering on the Platte. Beaver are found along some stretches, and there are many muskrat. Whitetail deer browse the area along the willow thickets of the river during the bitter winters. And at several places around Scotts Bluff along the Platte, the ruts worn in the hard rock by the many wagon trains that passed this way during the 1800s still are plainly visible. On nearby rock walls are carved the names and initials of many of those who rode the trains.

Miles to the north across the tallgrass prairie and the Nebraska sandhills, another stream runs parallel to the Platte—the Niobrara. Here one may find not only herds of bison, but one of the last remaining long-horned cattle herds which made western history during the era of the great cattle drives out of Texas and Oklahoma. Today they graze the grasslands of the Niobrara National Wildlife Refuge near Valentine, Nebraska.

By 1900 the great black tides of bison that roamed the grasslands had all but disappeared. By 1910 there were only an estimated one thousand left in the entire United States. Just two years later, J. W. Gilbert of Friend, Nebraska, offered to give six bison, seventeen elk, and several mule deer to the federal government if land could be made available on which to keep the animals. The land associated with the abandoned old Fort Niobrara was obtained for this purpose. Since then, it has been enlarged to comprise the present 19,122 acres of the refuge. The Niobrara River flows through it.

All of the prairie rivers are normally slow-moving and sluggish, but the outstanding example is perhaps the James, plodding some seven hundred miles through the Dakotas, dropping an average of only five inches per mile. The Jim, as it is locally called, is probably the longest unnavigable river in the United States.

The prairie rivers flow through a rugged landscape subject to sudden and merciless elements. The winds blow constantly across the sea of grass. In the southern portions a dry blast of summer may, within only a few days, parch everything in its path. A sudden norther may bring a cold front sweeping across the plains in hours; or moisture-laden air from the Gulf may dump ten inches of rain on the land overnight, turning the raw gullies and worn stream beds into raging torrents. Perhaps this direct and immediate relationship between land and water and weather best explains the simple beauty of so many prairie rivers.

9

HEARTLAND RIVERS

I thought in a panic, I shall never
be happy on land again. I was afraid once more
of all the painful circumstances of living.
But when the dry ground was under us,
the world no longer fluid,
I found a forgotten loveliness in all the things
that have nothing to do with men.
Beauty is pervasive, and fills, like perfume,
more than the object that contains it.
Because I had known intimately a river,
the earth pulsed under me.
—Marjorie Kinnan Rawlings

1. The mighty Father of Waters seemingly stretches forever, in both length and width. Even though it is one of the most polluted rivers in America along much of its course, it is also one of the most beautiful.

In a land of tamarack swamps, sphagnum bogs, and glacier lakes in northern Minnesota, a great river—the Father of Waters—is born. Escaping over a boulder-strewn fault in the embankment of Lake Itasca, the Mississippi begins a trek of more than two thousand miles to the Gulf of Mexico through the center of America. In the beginning it would seem as though it does not want to make the long journey, seeking instead a shorter route to the sea. First it heads north toward Hudson Bay, then turns east toward Lake Superior.

Perhaps at one time before the multiple glaciers carved their way through these North Woods, the Mississippi, if it existed at all, did indeed connect with other arteries leading to one of these bodies of water... or perhaps to both. But now, curbed by an immovable embankment of land and rock, it turns south near the city of Grand Rapids and gains momentum, seeking out the sea via America's heartland.

The Mississippi basin is vast, draining the fourth largest area of any river on earth—1.4 million square miles or 41 percent of the U.S. mainland excluding Alaska. It extends from the Potomac Highlands of West Virginia to western Montana and into Canada's Manitoba province. It is perhaps easier to grasp the extent of this drainage in terms of the tributaries of the Mississippi: the Ohio, Missouri, Red, Tennessee, or Arkansas. The Missouri alone, which joins the Mississippi near St. Louis, is nearly as long as the Mississippi itself—some 2,300 miles.

In its upper reaches, the Mississippi is pristine and wild, flowing through a land seemingly little touched by man. Once it passes Minnesota's Twin Cities—Minneapolis and St. Paul—it begins to take on a different character, however. For man has had great impact upon it, impounding with dams, filling it with sewage and debris, converting it to his own will. Below the Falls of St. Anthony, where the water level drops eighty feet within half a mile, the river technically becomes not a river, but instead a series of lakes impounded by Corps of Engineers dams guaranteed to maintain a navigable channel for the big towboats that push millions of tons of commercial materials up and down the river each year.

Much of the midsection of the river glides past rolling prairie country—Wisconsin, Iowa, Illinois, and Missouri. Tall bluffs rise from the river's edge, and hundreds of islands and shifting sandbars dot the surface. On south, it picks up the muddy waters of the Missouri and the polluted ones of the Ohio, then rolls through the cotton plantation country of Arkansas, Mississippi, and Tennessee to the marsh and swamplands of the low country.

The Mississippi is truly the father of waters to Louisiana, for it built the land. Once the sea jutted inland, but the great river, contributing silt from all over mid-America, kept building and building until the land arose above the water, pushing the coast farther and farther south.

Each year, the Atchafalaya, one of the streams that branches off the Mississippi near its mouth, carries

more than 130 million tons of sediment to the sea—adding three hundred yards to Louisiana's growing shore. And the Mississippi itself carries an estimated 685 million tons of sedimentary material to the Gulf each year, or an average daily load of more than 1.5 million tons. Even the city of New Orleans sits upon a layer of sediment seven hundred feet thick...and it's unstable. In fact, the city is sinking as the sediment becomes more compacted.

The silting and sediment action is a natural process. It was underway long before the European came to America, but it has been accelerated since that time by poor land practices and the stripping of timber from the land throughout the drainage area. The most environmentally damaging aspect, however, is that the water and sediment are often charged with toxic chemicals—insecticides from the farmlands and orchards, industrial wastes and acids from factories and mines. Many of them are not biodegradable and settle to the bottom to be picked up by tiny bacteria, thus entering the life chain again.

A case in point was the disappearance upon two different occasions in recent years of the brown pelican from coastal waters around the Mississippi delta. Louisiana, known traditionally as the Pelican State, for long periods has been without a single brown pelican resident. The pollutants did not affect the fish, but when the fish were consumed by the pelicans, the poison wiped them out, almost overnight. The pelican population was again established, and again it was annihilated. The poisons are often undetected by the human eye, but the swirling patterns of sediment deposits show up in high aerial views over the delta country. And those patterns are also the location of the toxic material.

The patterns are changing, however, for now the delta has reached nearly the edge of the continental shelf, and the spill of sediment-laden waters spews its burden farther and farther to sea. In so doing, the silt settles out in waters hundreds of feet deep; it would take millions of years before any discernable build-up would occur.

Much of that sediment carried down by the Mississippi comes, of course, from the muddy Missouri, which drains a more arid land subject to flash floods and rapid runoff. For quite some distance downstream after the two join, the Mississippi indeed looks like two rivers flowing side by side in the same channel. On one side the water flows relatively clear and blue; on the other, it is thick with reddish silt. Eventually, provoked by the wind and interreacting currents, the two streams mix, and the Mississippi remains muddy all the way to the Gulf.

Without the Ohio and the Missouri, the Mississippi would be only a comparative trickle emptying in the Gulf of Mexico. While the Missouri is perhaps the most interesting, flowing some 2,300 miles across mountains, plains, and prairies in ten states, it is the Ohio which delivers the greatest volume of water to the Mississippi. In fact, there are those who claim the Ohio is the major river; the Mississippi is merely a tributary of it. If you visit the point of land just south of Cairo, Illinois, where the two rivers meet, you're inclined to agree, for the Ohio is precisely twice as wide here as the Mississippi, and carries twice as much water as the Missouri and Mississippi combined. A full fourth of all the water pouring into the Gulf of Mexico from the Father of Waters actually comes from the Ohio.

But virtually all the heartland rivers, particularly the major ones, have been so altered by man that they only faintly resemble what they once were. Most have been converted into a chain of lakes by high dams. The main channels have been drowned by the raised water levels, banks eroded, bottomlands inundated, and plantlife destroyed. While some contend this has improved the river's capabilities for supporting wildlife and marine life, it nonetheless has altered the natural course of the streams, which may, in time, prove either good or bad. The fish habitat in most of the streams has actually improved within the last few years. Sturgeon, which require good quality water, are again showing up sporadically in the Ohio and Mississippi, and some say the ancient paddlefish, once found in great numbers in the Missouri and Mississippi, are again increasing.

At the turn of the century, paddlefish up to six feet long and weighing 150 pounds were taken from both the Mississippi and Missouri. But overfishing of these unique river giants and the damming of tributary streams where they spawned contributed most to their demise. They are now considered a rarity.

In its natural state, the lower Mississippi is a wandering gypsy stream; so is the Missouri. No one was ever sure where or when they might change direction, seek

3

2. *(Preceding page) La Belle Rivière...that's what the early Frenchmen called the Ohio. It funneled the westward movement of settlers down from Pittsburgh.*

3. *Johnny Appleseed once trekked westward through portions of the Ohio Valley, planting apple orchards. Some of those trees and their offspring still fill the air with the smell of blossoms.*

4. *Whitetail deer are plentiful along many of the heartland rivers.*

5. *The imperial moth.*

6. *The yellow-billed cuckoo, which feeds on tent caterpillars, among other things, is common in the Missouri and Ohio River valleys.*

4

5

6

7. *Along several of the heartland rivers are unusual geological formations. The one near the Ohio River in southern Illinois is called Garden of the Gods. It's in the Shawnee National Forest.*

8. *The effects of high waters show on these rocks in southern Ohio along the Ohio River.*

8

9

10

9. *A pair of deadly amanita mushrooms. Much of heartland America is great mushroom territory, for both toxic and edible varieties.*

10. *Virginia creeper, which many people mistake for poison ivy, grows along the forest floor.*

7

11. Mallard ducks, as well as dozens of other varieties, use the Mississippi flyway during fall and spring migrations.

12. A ladybug feeds upon a dandelion blossom.

13. Goldenrod against an autumn sky.

14. Among the tributaries of the Mississippi are the Tennesssee and Cumberland, which begin here in the mountains of Appalachia.

11

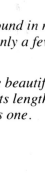

12

13

15. Squawroot, found in many parts of heartland America, grows only a few inches above the hardwood forest floor.

16. (Overleaf) The beautiful Ohio River, along the southern third of its length, still flows by pastoral scenes such as this one.

15

14

143

17

John Ebeling

18

17. *Winter brings a cloak of snow and ice to many of the heartland rivers, particularly those portions lying north of latitude 40.*

18. *River otters play in the snow along the upper Mississippi in Minnesota.*

19. *The snow waters that fall on the hills of the heartland river drainage will ultimately be carried off by the streams to subtropical climes.*

20. *A bubbling brook struggles against the encroaching sheet of ice.*

19

20

21

21. *Hen of the Woods, an edible mushroom.*

22. *In autumn the leaves of beech (shown here), maple, and poplar turn the woodlands to a soft gold.*

23. *Caesar's mushroom—orange amanita—is highly toxic.*

24. *The Angel of Death, another deadly amanita mushroom.*

25. *(Overleaf) In the Mississippi delta, where all heartland rivers end, the water disperses into a distributary marshland where river water mingles with that of the salty Gulf of Mexico.*

23

24

out a new bed and abandon the older one. Consequently in the lower Mississippi are many oxbow lakes which were cut off from the mainstream but which are kept alive and supplied by regular flooding.

Most of that natural action has ceased now, however, for the Corps of Engineers, in order to protect the interests of various commercial enterprises along the route, has built dikes, dams, and reinforced embankments so the river can no longer choose its own way.

The great river was considerably different back on June 17, 1673, when a French Jesuit missionary, Father Jacques Marquette, with Louis Jolliet, a Canadian fur trader, and five French boatmen paddled great Voyageur canoes down the Wisconsin River. Gliding along the left bank of the stream, they spotted a sandbar jutting from a steep bluff. Heavy clumps of golden willows obstructed their view beyond. Before reaching the sandbar, the cliff retreated to the left, and the current, now stronger, swept the craft from behind the willows and exposed suddenly a panorama that left them wondering if they were not seeing a mirage. For just in front of them opened up a magnificent river such as they had never seen before.

Marquette and Jolliet chose to follow it south; they were sure it would ultimately lead them to the Orient. But not finding this to be true, they became disenchanted with the great river and turned back. Far downriver, the Spanish had already explored the lower portions of the Mississippi; in fact, DeSoto died upon its banks near what is today Memphis. He is credited with the discovery of the river in 1539.

Regardless of its changes by man, the Mississippi and its tributaries remain an excellent habitat for wildlife. From its headwaters in northern Minnesota to the Gulf, the Mississippi is the greatest American flyway for migrating waterfowl. Canada geese, snow and blue geese, mallard, blue wing teal, and canvasbacks fill the skies during the months of October and November and again in the spring months of March and early April. On unoccupied islands along the river, bobcat and swamp rabbit and even coyotes and wolves still roam. Buffalo were once a common sight along the river, and whitetail deer are still common.

In the lower reaches of the river are alligator and great wading birds. The great blue heron is more associated with the entire length of the Mississippi than any other bird. Several rookeries are found along it, but they represent only a fraction of the number found in the 1930s and the 1940s. Bald eagles also fish the river, and during winter at a dam near Alton, Illinois, as many as one hundred eagles have been spotted at a single time perched in trees around the open pools just below the gates. They apparently gather there to fish in the turbulent water when the river is frozen at other places.

Even as much as the Mississippi has been altered by dams and flood controls, Old Muddy or Old Misery, as the Missouri is often called, has suffered even more. There are more than a thousand reservoirs on that river or its tributaries, and more are being planned. The Ohio has nineteen dams on it. And the Tennessee, major tributary to the Ohio, has been developed about as far as man can envision it through an agency that does not

150 even answer to Congress—the Tennessee Valley Au-

25

Lee Jenkins

26

Lee Jenkins

27

Lee Jenkins

28

26. *Along the Mississippi are several heron and egret rookeries, only a small percentage of those that were here 25 years ago. Here (top) is a common egret (white) and little blue heron, both nesting in the same area. (27.) A heron nest with three eggs, about the limit, is shown at lower left, while a baby little blue heron is at right. (28.) This particular rookery is located on an island in the river.*

thority. There are more than twenty TVA dams on the Tennessee; they produce electricity as well as provide flood control and recreation opportunities. Still others are planned, and one of these set off a controversy recently over a nearly extinct little fish called the snail darter. If the dam is constructed, the snail darter may disappear from the face of the earth.

All of the rivers in the Mississippi basin have had interesting and colorful histories. The Ohio became the major route west during one era, as flatboats and keelboats and virtually anything that would float brought settlers down from Pittsburgh (then Fort Pitt). Many settled at such places as Cincinnati, Louisville, and Evansville and old Shawneetown in Illinois. But the Missouri also played a role in the western movement, even though it flowed the wrong way and created many navigation hazards because of its fickle character and changing riverbed.

The largest boat traffic on Big Muddy was brought about by the discovery of gold in the Rockies at the end of the Civil War. Although the shallow-draft river steamers could only make it as far as the mouth of the Marias River, thousands of fortune hunters and hundreds of tons of freight were hauled upstream. Interest was renewed in that era in 1968 when one of the old river steamers—the *Bertrand*, which sank in 1865—was discovered buried in the bottomlands of the DeSoto National Wildlife Refuge near Omaha, Nebraska.

The Missouri River had covered the *Bertrand* with thirty feet of muck before changing its channel and leaving the boat a few hundred yards away. Excavations to determine the type of loot still on her uncovered some 150 tons of champagne, Bourbon whisky, exotic canned goods, and even such items as horse-drawn plows, bolts, and hobnailed shoes.

The *Bertrand* exemplifies the treacherous character of the Missouri, for it was just one boat that sank; there were over four hundred, most of them victims of treachery by the river itself. Despite markers and dredging activities on the stream to this day, boats still run aground on shifting sandbars. And just to confirm the position that she is not completely tamed, the Missouri occasionally lashes out with an unpredictable flood such as in 1973, the worst in 150 years.

But floods are not unusual in the Mississippi drainage, for hardly a year passes that some river within the system does not flood. The Ohio has run rampant upon several occasions, the worst flood in recent times taking place in 1937. The Corps of Engineers predicts what they term a "project" flood, the worst in Mississippi River history, by the year 2000, however. And even though they've been preparing for it for half a century, the Corps admits there is little they can do to protect the cities along the river against such a flood if it should occur.

The conquest of the Mississippi and its tributaries has been called one of the most ambitious undertakings ever conceived by man. But as one flies south from New Orleans and sees the mighty river disperse and disappear into a fan alluvial plain, one senses that our ingenuity is puny indeed when it comes to wrestling with Ol' Man River.

29

30

31

29, 30. One of the most fascinating geological formations along the heartland rivers occurs at Falls of the Ohio across from Louisville, Kentucky. Here is one of the finest examples of exposed Great Devonian Reef in North America. Note fossils imbedded in the stone. (31.) The river has continued working and grinding away the fossil beds, however, in places leaving only small potholes of water.

32. The river takes away and the river gives. Along the Ohio are huge piles of driftwood covering several acres, brought by high waters.

32

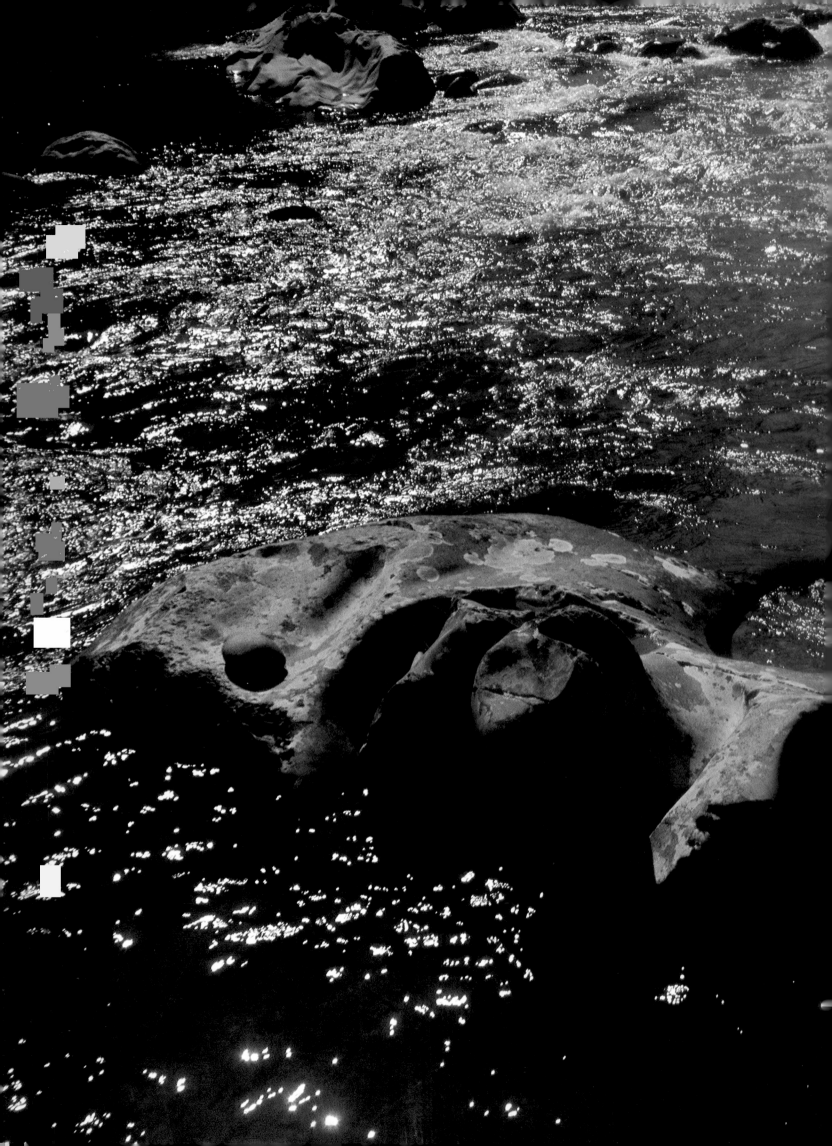

2. Several rivers are born in the Potomac Highlands of West Virginia. They flow in different directions and end their journey half a continent away.

3. Wild bean.

4. In the high country along many of the mountain rivers grow apples; in springtime they give the slopes a luster of white blossoms.

3

4

2

From the backbone of eastern America—a great range of mountains extending from New York's Adirondacks near the Canadian border down to northern Georgia—spring a multitude of streams flowing in several directions. We shall call that area Appalachia; the streams to which it gives sustenance are the rivers of the eastern mountains.

The most interesting among them is the huge Hudson, which rises in the Adirondacks not far from the Canadian border, but the rivers of the eastern mountains also include what many consider our national river—the Potomac—and such buccaneering streams as the Chattooga, the Tallulah, the Obed of Tennessee, the Cheat, the Delaware, the Natalaha, the Younghiohery, the Monogahela, and that river of history—the Susquehanna.

A legend is told in the mountains of West Virginia about a barn standing near Spruce Knob in the Potomac Highlands which sheds water into three great river systems—the Potomac, the James, and the Ohio. While this barn may actually exist only in legend, it is not improbable that such a spot could be found at many points of the Appalachian Highlands. For this is a place where rivers are born; what direction they flow is immaterial.

The Catskills, the Blue Ridge, the Poconos, the Alleghenies, and the Great Smokies: these are collectively the fir-thatched roof of eastern America. Eastward the mountains slope to the Piedmont, westward to the interior plateau and the Mississippi Valley. The valley and ridge pattern extends one thousand miles from northern Alabama to Lake Champlain; its widest point is seventy five miles in Pennsylvania.

Named for an Indian tribe, the Apalachees, the mountains provided a formidable barrier that thwarted westward movement in the United States for nearly two centuries after Spanish explorations in the south, a century after the European came to the eastern seashore. Only when Daniel Boone blazed a trail through Cumberland Gap between North Carolina, Tennessee, and Kentucky in 1775 did the bottle become uncorked and humanity flow to the undeveloped lands of the west—more than 300,000 of them in a quarter of a century.

The Appalachians are old; their rocky links began to take shape more than four hundred million years ago. And then they were subjected to the forces of the great glaciers. Several of them pushed into the ranges, the last one occurring some twenty thousand years ago. It is this one that left its impressions most clearly imprinted in the landscape, for it all but erased the traces of earlier ones. Long before the glaciers, during an era when the mountains were part of a drowned continent, much of the basic Appalachian geology was formed, a geology that during recent times has given the nation great wealth in coal and oil. Unfortunately, no part of the nation has suffered more from the industrial process than this chain of mountain ranges and the rivers that flow from them. Many of the rivers are so polluted, including the Potomac, that even swimming is discouraged.

Yet upstream near the Potomac's source on the South Branch in West Virginia, the water is clean enough to

5

6

5. *This tiny fawn comes to drink the waters of the Susquehanna in Pennsylvania's high country.*

6. *Although the Potomac is clear enough to drink near its headwaters in West Virginia, by the time it reaches the Falls of the Potomac just outside Washington, D.C., it is heavily polluted with silt, chemicals, and bacteria.*

7. *Fall in the hardwood forest of the high country.*

7

drink. It's the same with the Hudson, the Delaware, the Monongahela, and the Allegheny. Most of the pollution comes from human sewage and the waste man has carelessly tossed aside, from the chemicals used in factories and on farmlands, from the muddy silt washed down from the strip mines and coal deposits and over-cropped, eroded fields.

Enough evidence still exists of the streams' once pristine qualities to hold dreams and hopes of a new day, however, when these mountain streams will again flow sweet and free. In fact, one has only to look at such rivers as the Chattooga and certain portions of the Tallulah in mountainous Georgia, or indeed at the upper Hudson shortly after it begins in the Adirondacks or the Potomac in the Potomac Highlands of West Virginia, to realize what an eastern mountain river should be like.

Perhaps more streams have suffered from pollution from coal strip-mining than from any other form in the Appalachian Highlands, especially in West Virginia, Kentucky, Pennsylvania, Tennessee, and Virginia. Kentucky State Representative Harry Caudill put it:

Imagine a heavily forested ridge with its second growth of hickories, oaks, tulip poplars, beeches, and gums. Imagine a knee-high carpet of ferns and other low-growing ground cover. Populate it with whole communities of rabbits, squirrels, foxes, serpents, and many other animals and reptiles. Count the birds of many species that nest and twitter in the branches. Consider the grubs, snails, worms, moles, and other creatures that live in the soil itself and in rotting logs, heaps of leaves, and under stones.

Then visualize the coal strippers at work upon this silent empire of interrelated plants and creatures. The biggest earth-moving equipment in existence roars and rumbles as their massive treads grind into the woodland, toppling trees and moving the mountain . . . every creature that inhabits the forest has been slain or put to flight. The mountain has been destroyed, the forests that clothe it are gone, the streams that flow from its drainage ruined.

Precious minerals played a role along the Potomac at one time, too, but it was not ruined by the strip-mining process; all of the minerals were underground. Gold was first discovered in the vicinity of the Falls of the Potomac just minutes upstream from Washington, D.C., in 1861. Several mines were opened on the Maryland side of the river and mining continued off and on for a number of years. The mines finally closed at the begining of World War II mainly because the ceiling price on gold in this country made operations improfitable. The late E. T. Ingalls, who for many years was foreman at one of the mines, claimed shortly before his death in the early 1970s that rich veins of ore still were located near the surface at the falls. But now the National Park Service, which operates the Chesapeake & Ohio Canal National Historic Park, owns the mines and it's unlikely any mining will ever be done there again

The gold veins, estimated by the U.S. Geological Survey to run no more than a quarter of a mile wide at right angles to the course of the river, likely were created from great pressure exercised on the schist and graywacke rock during a period of folding and diking of the earth at this point. All this probably happened **159**

8

9

10

11

12

8. *Evidence of the constant grinding power of the mountain rivers is demonstrated by these potholes in an abandoned stream bed in the Smoky Mountains National Park.*

9. *The dashing Tallulah River in Georgia's mountains is among the most beautiful mountain streams of the East.*

10. *Throughout much of Appalachia, the rhododendren grows as forest understory.*

11. *During early summer, beautiful blossoms of the wild hydrangea, or hobblebush, decorate the riverbank.*

12. *Mountain pink phlox grows in cracks between the rocks along the Chattooga River.*

13. *(overleaf) Morning fog lies heavy in the steep mountain valleys of the Appalachian high country.*

14

16

14. *Along the Tallulah River, a fly honeysuckle vine climbs the rock cliffs.*

15. *A small mountain stream in a hurry.*

16. *Mountain laurel, common along many mountain streams.*

15

Bill Deane

17

18

17. *A cluster of nine pink lady's-slippers.*

18. **Buckleya distichophylla** *growing along the upper Hudson.*

19. *The Palisades of the Hudson, not far upstream from Manhattan, are an imposing geological formation; they are more than 300 feet high and they border the river for many miles.*

20. *(Overleaf) The upper reaches of the Potomac, America's national river, in the Potomac Highlands of West Virginia.*

19

during the Ordovician (440 million years ago) and the Devonian Period (370 million years ago). The same movement created the geological base which later became the Falls of the Potomac.

Miles upstream in the mountains, where the Potomac begins, acid from old mining wastes still flows into the river, rendering it far less fertile than it should be. Acid has been the curse of the North Branch of the Potomac since coal was first discovered on one of its tributaries, Georges Creek, in 1782. Most of the mines are inactive now, but in their dark recesses water reacts with pyrites and air, forming sulfuric acid and other noxious brews that the old shafts spew out into creeks. Often the stream beds become coated with garish, toxic mineral salts known to miners as "yellow boy." Virtually nothing will live in these waters, not even a single bacterium that normally cleanses streams of pollution.

But the Potomac has marvelous resiliency; it cleans itself within a few miles as other streams, not suffering pollution, enter and dilute its troubled waters. By the time the Potomac gets to the nation's capital, or to the Falls, it contains a much higher quality water. At Washington the river is injected again with poisons of a dozen different kinds. Again it cleanses itself, however, becoming a fecund environment for oysters and numerous species of salt-water fish.

For 382 of its winding miles, the Potomac forms the border between Maryland and Virginia. Bypassing some mountains and cutting through others, it bursts through the Blue Ridge, then wanders across the Piedmont and the Shenandoah Valley, past such historical places as Antietam and Harper's Ferry, parallels from Cumberland, Maryland, to Washington the old Chesapeake and Ohio Canal that was George Washington's dream for a waterway west from the Chesapeake to the Ohio River.

Years ago, the fish in the Potomac in the Washington area were put off limits to people who would eat them, and, later, signs were posted warning people not to enter the river. It was unsafe even for swimming. President Lyndon B. Johnson ordered a cleanup that will continue for years. He called the Potomac "truly the American river" and proposed an ambitious development and recreation program that would have formally created the Potomac National River. Nothing ever came of these plans, but the cleanup does continue.

Much of the Potomac upstream from Washington today gives the distinct impression of wilderness. Along its banks sway huge sycamores, cottonwoods, maples, and willows above floodplain floors carpeted in spring with trilliums and dandelions. It flows through dense stands of forest and sporadic wetlands filled with the songs of warblers and goldfinches, robins and mockingbirds. Occasionally the squawk of the great blue heron or the cackling of the little green breaks the silence, while from overhead comes the shrill cry of the red-tailed hawk. Deer browse the mountains, and in West Virginia and western Maryland wild turkey haunt the forest. Bobcat are said to exist there, too, and along the South Branch are dwindling numbers of black bear.

Few rivers anywhere can compare in natural or **167**

geological interest to the mighty Hudson, which is born at Lake Tear of the Clouds on Mount Marcy in the Adirondacks and flows past Manhattan to join the sea at Lower Bay. Once it flowed onward across the Continental Shelf another 120 miles before meeting the Atlantic and, enroute, carved a canyon 120 feet and sometimes two miles wide. That was during the Great Ice Age of Pleistocene times, but after the ice melted, thereby raising the ocean's water level, the canyon drowned. Today it is a major habitat for a multitude of fish and marine life.

Extending now only 315 miles, the Hudson is often considered not as a single river but as a series of interconnecting streams, each continuing where the other ends. Near the headwaters, the Hudson is a fine trout stream and you can drink the water directly from the stream; next it becomes a bass and pike river, a canal, a septic tank at Albany, and ultimately an estuary and seaport at New York City. The lower portion is actually not a river at all but an arm of the sea—some call it a fjord—fluctuating with the tides. The ebb and flow of salt water and fresh water interacting upon one another extends all the way to Albany at times. The river is saltier near the bottom, as the fresh mountain water coming down from the Adirondacks tends to ride on top of the salt water, being lighter than the water burdened with salt.

While the salt content in the water varies from time to time, depending on the flow of fresh water down the Hudson, it usually accounts for about twenty-three parts per thousand at Manhattan's Battery Park; at Bear Mountain, it runs about five.

This mixing of salt and fresh water in the lower Hudson presents some interesting marine situations, allowing both fresh-water fish and ocean species to share the same stream. Usually the fresh-water fishes stay closer to the surface and the salt varieties near the bottom where the higher salinities exist. Harbor seals have traveled upstream as far as Troy, 154 miles from the mouth.

During normal water flow when there have been no heavy rains upstate, the flow of the Hudson downstream from Albany is equivocal. A stick tossed into the river at the state capital might drift ten miles downriver and nine back up. This is quite in contrast to the era when the last great glacier was melting. The Hudson then was the feeder stream from the Great Lakes which poured an unbelievable volume of water down the valley. The Hudson then reached from high hill to high hill, mountain to mountain. It was during this time when it eroded away the great canyon extending across the Continental Shelf. The St. Lawrence eventually stole away the flow from the Great Lakes, however, and the Hudson waters diminished.

Biologically and botanically, the Hudson and its valley are rich. The biological productivity of the lower Hudson, despite its pollution with PCBs, sewage, and other chemical wastes, is indeed staggering. Fish are there by the millions. Sea sturgeon, striped bass, bluefish, shad, herring, largemouth bass, carp, yellow perch, needlefish, menhaden, darters, sunfish, tomcod, and golden shiners all are to be found in the lower

Hudson. Also found here is the round-nosed sturgeon, classified by the Department of the Interior as an endangered species.

Dr. Alistair McCrone, a geologist at New York University who has done extensive studies on the Hudson, says that the rich variety of marine life is due partly to a surprising number of minerals deposited on the floor of the river, minerals which help to provide nutrients. Dr. McCrone found the water contains a variety of ions derived from such minerals as antimony, boron, calcium, chromium, copper, magnesium, aluminum, nickel, silicon, titanium, beryllium, and zirconium. Vast populations of bacteria act upon these nutrients, and thus begins the chain of life.

When a plant or animal dies, the smaller creatures of the deep feed upon it. Bacteria, eels, shrimp, crabs, and other scavengers help to recycle the nutrients. The action of the tides and the flow from the north activates the lower river until it is like a great rocking chair, constantly stirring its contents, thoroughly mixing them. The result is vibrant life.

That vibrant life continues onto the land. Many southern species of birds and animals have moved into the Hudson Valley during the past two centuries. The Carolina wren, which normally requires a warm climate, now lives in the cliffs of the Hudson Palisades in New Jersey, which tower 525 feet above the river. The fence lizard, the opossum and raccoon, the Canada warbler, the white-tailed deer, the river otter, mink, and even beaver are inhabitants of the Hudson Valley.

The Hudson, of course, could only legitimately be considered a mountain river down as far as Albany; beyond that it begins to change dramatically, even though the plum-toned Catskills to the west are still within sight. Then the hills begin to move closer until they rear up sharply over the river around the community of Newburgh. This area is known as the Highlands, and its fifteen miles are the least spoiled section of the lower river. Here, at a jut of land called World's End, just across from the ramparts of West Point, the river plunges to its greatest depth of 216 feet. In sight of that spot, just two miles upstream, Storm King Mountain soars 1,300 feet almost straight up with the bulk and suggestion of violence that make it resemble a bear.

No other river of Appalachia is quite like the Hudson here. Other rivers cut scenically through the mountains; only the Hudson does it without rising above sea level. Shortly do2nstream from here—at the Tappan Zee—it reaches its widest point: 3.3 miles.

Long before there were river systems as we know them today, the prehistoric Teays River flowed north out of the Appalachians toward the depression which would someday become the Great Lakes. Remnants of that river still may be found today—the New River of West Virginia follows its general path. The Teays was old before the Rocky Mountains were born. Time and the elements have changed the face of the continent. In place of the vanished Teays came such rivers as the Ohio and the Mississippi, but the mountains which fostered the Teays still live, and are still the source of dozens of rivers flowing in various directions from the summit of eastern America.

22

21. *Sharp-lobed hepatica on a moss and lichen covered cliff.*

22. *The yellow russula mushroom.*

21

23

24

23. Seneca Creek, a tributary of the South Branch of the Potomac, is an excellent West Virginia mountain trout stream.

24. The Hudson, shortly before reaching the sea, features marshy estuaries built by silting and current action. Waterfowl and songbirds nest here.

25. Thomas Jefferson once described this view of the Potomac from Harper's Ferry, West Virginia, as being worth a trip across the Atlantic.

25

11

LAND LOCKED RIVERS OF THE GREAT BASIN

Here one may sit upon the riverbank
pondering the edge of immortality and wonder
where the water went.
—Anonymous

1. Born at Lake Tahoe in the high Sierras, the
imprisoned Truckee River flows quietly through
pristine forests and bordering marshlands before
finding its way to the floor of the Nevada desert.

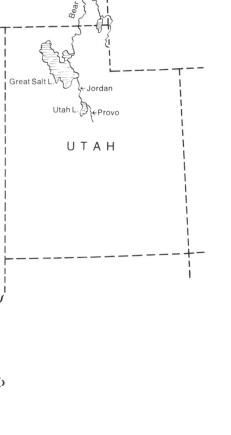

2. Much of the territory through which the landlocked rivers flow is a desert of mesquite and creosote bush, seemingly devoid of life.

Seven huge white pelicans soared overhead, then glided in formation down to the water glimmering like a mirage against the purple mountains of the Stillwater range. Sandpipers, spindly-legged avocets, and common egrets were everywhere, picking morsels from the marine life of the shallows. The bulrushes and cattails rustled in the light breeze, and the desert beyond danced with heat waves. The place was the Humboldt Sink, where a river dies.

The Humboldt River, which wends its way across most of the state of Nevada, is one of the primary Great Basin rivers. It wages continuous battle for survival, for everywhere it goes the land is thirsty. The Humboldt Sink lies fan-shaped upon the Nevada desert just east of Reno along busy Interstate 80. Three miles up the road is the small town of Lovelock. But there is little evidence of man in the Humboldt Sink. It is a wild place, the domain of the osprey, the coyote, and the beaver. The Humboldt River disappears here, evaporating into the desert air.

The Humboldt generally is not a beautiful stream. The sparse growth along its banks marks a ragged path in the desert. Stunted willows at the water's edge give way to mesquite and sagebrush a few feet away from the bank. Dust devils created by the hot winds dislodge debris and grains of dust and sand as they track a playful zig-zag mile across the desert before coming abruptly to the narrow Humboldt, where they suddenly lose momentum and die, dropping their burden into the shallow waters. And the river, slowly but relentlessly, carries away the dust.

Except for the first few miles from its origin in the Jarbridge, Ruby, and Independence mountains, the Humboldt is a flat-surface, slow-moving, lazy desert stream with an almost imperceptible current. As a crow flies, it's only three hundred miles from beginning to end, but the Humboldt meanders a thousand miles on its course, making it the longest American river within the boundaries of one state. Rarely is it more than thirty feet across and four or five feet deep, usually less.

Once it leaves the mountains, where it is actually a sparkling clear mountain stream, it gains virtually no support from rain. A few sluggish tributaries join to give it momentum and life in the upper reaches but soon there is nothing but an occasional dry wash along its path. And the river, instead of becoming larger and larger as with most streams elsewhere, becomes smaller and smaller. Eventually, the hot sun and the thirsty desert have robbed it of life until, at the Humboldt Sink, it can travel no farther. Spreading out upon the desert which thus far has contained it, the waters evaporate into the atmosphere to be deposited again upon the land, perhaps to become a part of another river.

The Humboldt is indeed an unusual river, but so are all the rivers of the Great Basin—the Truckee, the Owens, the Walker, the Jordan, the Bear, to name but a few. They are unique in that none of them ever find the sea. From the time a river is born, it is searching out the ocean. But the rivers of the Great Basin are all landlocked streams. They are born, run for awhile, then either end abruptly in a lake or vanish into thin air as does the Humboldt.

Over the mountains in California, the Owens River winds its way through another arid region near the Sierras. The Paiute Indians once worshiped the river as a gift from the gods. It still is, but the gift is now in dispute between a handful of people in the Owens Valley, who depend upon it as a life-sustaining artery, and the people of Los Angeles, who have drained away much of it to fill swimming pools and water lawns.

Like an indigo snake on a beige carpet, the Owens emerges onto the floor of a mountain corridor on the almost forgotten eastern side of California. For more than eighty miles the river runs parallel to the Sierra Nevada; to the east lie the arid White and Inyo Mountains crowned with bristlecone pines, most ancient of all living things. At its narrowest point, the valley is less than twenty miles across from one crest to another with 14,000-foot peaks on both sides. Mt. Whitney, rising to 14,494 feet—the highest in the lower forty-eight states—stands just west of the Owens. To the east and southeast and south lie Death Valley and the Mojave Desert.

The diversion of the Owens has imposed considerable hardships upon the valley's ranchers and farmers. More than 150 million gallons on an average day are pumped through the great aqueducts; environmentalists say that this situation threatens frail desert plants and that what wildlife does still exist will either perish or leave, including a rare black toad found in the marshes around Deep Springs Lake, an alkali smudge in the mountain-rimmed desert basin.

Occasionally a bald or golden eagle soars over the valley, riding the thermals down from the high country, searching for signs of life along the river. There are fewer eagles now as the years tick past, for there is less wildlife and fish life for them to feed upon.

Originally the Owens found its source in Lake Crawley, which survives from the snow waters flowing down from the mountains. But since 1970 when Los Angeles tunneled through a mountain to tap into Mono Lake, siphoning its waters into Lake Crawley and the Owens River, one would have to say the waters of the Owens now flow from that lake. Mono Lake, with Oz-like towers of tufa, a pockmarked limestone formation, is one of the most scenic in the state, but it too is now being drained away. The water level has dropped thirty feet since the aqueduct tapped into its basin, and the lake is now lifeless except for brine shrimp eaten by a tumult of seagulls and an occasional white pelican.

On the other end of the Owens River—where it once terminated—is Owens Lake, whose sand and gravel bed today is rippled only by the winds. No water ever reaches it. And yet once steamers hauled ore across its placid waters.

Streams of the Great Basin vary widely, of course. Much of the Truckee, for instance, is a mountain stream. It runs for miles toward Donner Pass after leaving Lake Tahoe before turning on itself and seeking a lower level toward the Nevada desert floor. The Truckee, Walker, and Carson rivers all find their source in the melting snows of the Sierra Nevada.

Along the way, the Truckee runs smack through the middle of Reno, the only large city on its hundred-mile route. During earlier days, before it reached the desert,

178

3

5

3. Some landlocked rivers end in lakes, but the Humboldt dies in the Humboldt Sink, which teems with wildlife. At first the sink appears to be a marsh, then becomes a land of sporadic potholes and ultimately only wet puddles on the desert. Note the beaver house here.

4. Among the interesting creatures of the landlocked rivers is the Western Grebe, shown here on Utah's Provo River. Although weak fliers, they are adept at catching small aquatic animals.

5. Its banks no longer containing it, the Humboldt spreads over the Nevada desert and dissipates into the thin, hot air.

6. (Overleaf) A marshy section of the Humboldt Sink. In the background is the Stillwater Mountain Range.

4

7

7. *One of the creatures found in the Humboldt Sink is the long-billed dowitcher, which feeds off the shallow bottom of the marsh. Usually found in small flocks, they make a single thin, peeping sound when approached.*

8. *Here in one of the deeper portions of the Humboldt Sink, the waters appear to be an extension of the Nevada sky.*

9. *The American avocet, common around many lakes and marshes of the west, is a summer visitor along several of the landlocked rivers of the Great Basin.*

8

9

connecting ponds were built along its course where ice could form during the winter months. The ice was carved by hand, then hauled by team and wagon to be stored and used for cooling during the hot summer months. And in the late 1800s, the Truckee served as a highway for logs on their way from the mountains to the railroad or to lumber mills. Much of it remains a beautiful rainbow and cutthroat trout stream to this day, with excellent water quality until it reaches Reno, which contributes to its pollution. Continuing north across the Nevada Desert, it soon comes to Pyramid Lake, which contains the largest nesting white pelican colony in North America. More than ten thousand birds nest here. It is also the only known habitat of the prehistoric Cui-ui (Qee-we) fish.

The Great Basin is a spectacular place. As late as 1750 it was still unknown to pioneers, and thereafter it discouraged development by man because of its generally arid condition. It was the last remaining frontier in the lower forty-eight states. Encompassing an area of approximately 210,000 square miles, it measures 880 miles in length from north to south and nearly 572 miles in width at its broadest point.

In spite of its name, the Great Basin is not a single saucer-like depression surrounded by mountains. Instead, it is a series of more than ninety basins separated from each other by more than 160 mountain ranges varying in length from thirty to 150 miles. The higher basin ranges reach altitudes varying from sea level in the southwest to four thousand to five thousand feet in the north. Many of these inner basins have their own interior drainage, and thus playa lakes, shallow sheets of water which cover many square miles during the winter but evaporate during the summer, are formed on the floor.

Although the Great Basin actually has many drainage basins in it, two huge ones—Bonneville and Lahontan —are primary. These were carved out by long tongues of ice during the Pleistocene period and were left as lakes when the ice melted about thirty-five thousand years ago. Bonneville Lake Basin drained about fifty-four thousand square miles in northern and western Utah, portions of Idaho, Wyoming, and Nevada. At its highest stage, the lake possessed an intricate shoreline which was a succession of promontories and deep bays; one may see evidence of it today a thousand feet above the present level of Great Salt Lake, which, along with Utah Lake, is all that remains of Lake Bonneville.

Four of the Great Basin landlocked rivers converge on Great Salt Lake to this day—the Ogden, Jordan, Weber, and Bear. Were it not for the tremendous amount of evaporation, the lake would soon be pressed to overflowing within a few days. Another landlocked stream—the Provo—flows down from the Wasatch Mountains through the city of Provo, Utah, to empty into Utah Lake.

Because of the meager amount of rainfall in the Great Basin, plantlife is stunted and sporadic. Broad plains and hills gray with sagebrush and shadscale are interspersed with scanty stands of juniper and piñon pine. **184** Southward, as precipitation decreases, plantlife is

nearly nonexistent, giving way to barren gravelly wastes dotted with scattered scrubs of creosote bush, greasewood and cacti, yucca and Joshua tree.

Large animals have always been scarce in the Great Basin area except for the higher mountain slopes, where there are bear, mountain lion, bighorn sheep, and mule deer. Antelope are found in the lower levels of the basin, as well as jackrabbit, a variety of snakes, lizards, and horned toads of the desert. Once buffalo ranged this far west, and notations by early travelers in the 1820s to 1840s noted sightings, especially along the Bear River. Beaver still work many of the rivers, and both muskrat and beaver are the primary engineers of the Carson and Humboldt sinks. The beaver build holding dams forming little pools and the muskrat tunnel between them, running the waters from one to another.

For many people, the sinks are the most interesting parts of the rivers, for here the river no longer is contained within banks, but spreads across the land, forming little holes and mud puddles everywhere. The desert sun soon evaporates those; what it does not, the land absorbs. Large cracks form, baked hard by the sun and subsequent water flowing into them disappears into the subterranean world. Willows and other waterborne shrubs grow profusely, making a sink appear as something of an oasis, but the growth is never thick enough to protect the water or the soil from the hot sun.

The Great Basin rivers are indeed a phenomenon in their own right, rich in history and possessed of subtle beauty. Yet there is a certain sadness in the thought of a stream, finding no strength apart from its own waters, that cannot find its way to the sea.

10. Bridal Veil Falls along the Provo River in Utah attracts thousands of tourists annually; some claim it's the most scenic spot along any Great Basin River.

11. The Truckee River seemingly disappears into the ground in this photograph. Actually, it's flowing into a sharp bend here, obscured by the camera angle; but some Great Basin streams do indeed drop abruptly out of sight in just such a manner.

12. A wide bed of well-worn stones has been laid down by the Truckee over eons of time; now they help to filter and clean the river during high water as well as hold the soil along the banks in place.

12

RIVERS
OF
THE DEEP
SOUTH

Any wild place is filled
with incredible things happening.
—David Cavagnaro/*This Living Earth*

*1. One of the most beautiful rivers of the South is
the Suwannee, bordered with cypress swamps
and fed by great crystal springs.*

Across the lower latitudes of America is a land laced with slow-moving waters; lazy rivers seemingly unsure or careless about their destinations. They set the pace—indeed, the atmosphere—for a place and a people. Along their banks wild azaleas, dogwood, redbud, and wild honeysuckle sweeten the spring air, and the wind sighs through groves of long-leaf pine.

Some of the rivers of the deep South are blackwater streams like the Suwannee; others, such as the Peace and Ichnetucknee of central Florida, run with the clarity of fine wine; still others—the Pearl and Pascagoula— flow much of the time with the consistency of thin mud as they drain the red clay hill farms and piney woods of Alabama, Mississippi, and Louisiana.

Because they run slowly and meander, for the most part, through areas of sparse population, these rivers are not streams of great destruction. Their waters may run high but seldom outside the normal flow patterns. The Suwannee, for instance, normally floods only once every twenty years. Many of the residents along its wilderness course can almost predict the exact time the high waters will come.

Perhaps it is the Suwannee which most fulfills one's expectations of a southern river. Stephen Foster composed a song that would immortalize the Suwannee, yet there are several historians who claim Foster never saw the stream. He chose it because the name to him possessed a romantic mystique and because of descriptions

given to him by people who had seen the Suwannee—a lazy, meandering blackwater stream ambling toward the Gulf through dense groves of live oak draped with Spanish moss, past swamps and great clearwater springs from the immense Floridian aquifer. Cypress knees crowded close along its banks, common egrets and great herons fed along its periphery, alligators and cottonmouth snakes bathed on the sandbars or in the shallow waters of the adjacent swamplands. During the time Foster wrote about it, a number of plantations had been developed along the upper Suwannee, but many later failed. And today the Suwannee, along at least two-thirds of its course, has all the appearances of a wilderness stream.

Enroute out of the great Okefenokee swamp, where it rises, the Suwannee flows through a chain of beautiful emerald lakes, all formed during dry periods when the peat bottom of the swamp dried out and caught fire, creating vast depressions. These later filled with water and are now lined with bonnet lilies, golden club, and bladderwort. The river also winds through natural channels created by large islands that provide a home and dry land for deer, black bear, bobcat, alligators, raccoons, opossum, wild turkey, and, some say, the endangered Florida panther.

On the Suwannee's journey through the swamp, its spongy banks sometimes melt away, and the river for a time becomes a part of a vast wetland surrounding it.

188

2. (Preceding page) The Peace River, with its emerald reflections of cypress and tupelo gum, is a favorite canoe stream in south Florida.

3. A flowering water lily floats on the dark waters of the Suwanee River near its source in Georgia's Okefenokee Swamp.

4. Greater celadine.

5. Water hyacinths, an exotic plant which has been found to have remarkable purifying qualities, are trapped by a fossil-imbedded limestone rock on the Oklawaha River.

6. Bunches of water lettuce, tugged away by the water, drift down the Peace River.

5

4

6

7

7. *A spider lily offers a late winter touch of beauty to the Oklawaha.*

8. *Many southern rivers are fed by springs. Here Manatee Springs empties into the Suwannee.*

9. Phlox drummondii.

8

9

10

11

12

10. *Many art forms are found along the river—pieces sculptured by nature such as this dead cypress.*

11. *Even the live cypress offers a unique art study; knees protruding from the water's edge as well as exposed roots form a net to collect debris from the water.*

12. *The cypress tree is more common than any other along many southern rivers, for it thrives in shallow water. The knees shown protruding above the water's surface are something of a mystery; no conclusive explanation of their role in the life-cycle of the tree has yet been established.*

But in periods of drought, water is found only in 'gator holes and in the main channel of the river. The Suwannee has been dammed just as it is about to leave the Okefenokee to maintain a stable water level in the swamp. But at no other place along its course have its waters suffered impoundment.

At some time in the past—mostly around the turn of the last century—thousands of cedar logs were cut along the Suwannee and floated downriver to market. Trees of other kinds and masses of underbrush in the valley change with the seasons, shading from pale greens through yellows and reds to dusky brown, but the cedars remain much the same the year around. Bass, perch, catfish and bream are found in small numbers in the river; small game is plentiful along its banks.

The dark color of the waters originates in the Okefenokee, where the trees and decaying vegetation leach a chemical called tannin into the stream. Tannin in excessive amounts can sterilize water and certainly limits the growth of microscopic life in the Suwannee, which, in turn, has a detrimental effect upon higher forms of aquatic life. Consequently, the Suwannee is not and has never been a great producer of fish.

Many of the rivers of the deep south, and particularly those in Florida, are born or are supplemented by great springs. As the spring water enters, the blackwater of the Suwannee fades. And then other tributaries—the Santa Fe, the Withlacoochee and Alapaha—join to broaden the Suwannee to a formidable width.

The springs themselves are worthy of special attention, for along the Suwannee and Oklawaha rivers are some of the greatest springs on the North American continent. Manatee Springs near Chiefland, Florida, for instance, rises from a bowl and pours more than forty-nine thousand gallons of water per minute into the nearby Suwannee. Up until the 1940s, the manatee or sea cow frequently came up the river to the springs, but rarely do they visit now. The sea cow, an endangered brackish water species, resembles in some ways a sea lion, but they have no tusks and are docile and harmless. They have a lotus-diet, range around ten feet in length, and may weigh 1,200 pounds or more. Marine biologists estimate there are only about one thousand in U.S. waters; they frequent the springs because of the warmer water temperatures in winter and because of the lush vegetation for food.

Along the east bank of the Suwannee five miles from Beel is Rock Bluff Springs, surrounded by enormous cypress trees, and near Old Town is Fanning Springs. Not all the springs belch clear water from the earth. Some springs are so laden with iron they are orange and their waters smell of sulphur. Along their run for the Suwannee, they deposit spongy masses of ironlike scum upon the landscape. No aquatic life lives within this scum.

At one time, the Suwannee marked the boundary between the territories of two Indian nations—the Timucua and the Apalachee; it was known to them as the Guasaca Esqui, or River of Reeds. The Spanish explorer Narvaez crossed it in 1528 and DeSoto in 1539; the latter christened it the River of the Deer. Indian guides led early Spanish explorers to believe its **195** waters flowed over beds of gold; thus contributing to its color. But geologic reports do not bear this out.

On the Oklawaha River a few miles to the south, gold never was part of the charm, but shells here and along the broad St. Johns, of which the Oklawaha is a tributary, attracted collectors. Great mounds of shells are found in the St. Johns, and in some instances they have created islands. Most of the shells are from various types of snails and mussels, and in earlier days Indians came here to gather the crustaceans for food.

The Oklawaha is a small, pristine river flowing through Florida's midsection. Much of its drainage territory is now contained in the Ocala National Forest, a pine and cypress woodland where lives one of the greatest concentrations of southern bald eagles. Studies by wildlife biologists are being carried out on fifty-six active eagle nests within a few miles of the Oklawaha and St. Johns rivers, and most of them produce young year after year.

13

Fed by springs bubbling up from the underlying limestone Ocala dome aquifer—the largest single water storage in the United States—the Oklawaha rises in several large lakes near the center of the Florida peninsula. A third of the way along its course, it is swelled by the tremendous outflow from Silver Springs, which pours some five hundred million gallons of water a day into it. Now vulgarized by commercial development, Silver Springs was once the most beautiful of all the great springs in Florida.

The country of the Ocala near the Oklawaha was the scene for Marjorie Kinnan Rawlings' novel, *The Yearling;* west of the Oklawaha lies the town she made famous in *Cross Creek*. But she was not the only writer impressed by this landscape. Sidney Lanier wrote the classic account of a trip on the Oklawaha in the opening chapter of his *Florida,* published ten years after the close of the Civil War, and naturalist William Bartram wrote great passages about the river during his sojourns in the Florida wilderness in the early 1800s.

In a land grossly impoverished by pollution of every form, the Oklawaha to this day remains largely free of pollution. From the air it is a thin black thread weaving through an interminable jungle of green, but from a boat it has less definable boundaries. The current runs not between banks of solid earth but through a winding avenue of trees knee-deep in water.

Osprey, eagles, red-tailed hawks, anhingas, great blue and little blue herons, common egrets—all are residents of the Oklawaha and its environs. And periodically from behind the green curtain of the palmetto jungle comes the forlorn cry of the limpkin, which thrives on the apple snail. Marjorie Rawlings described the Oklawaha as "one of the...last remaining haunts of this strange brown crane who cries before the rain."

The Pascagoula River, which empties into the Gulf of Mexico near the town of Pascagoula, Mississippi, is an unusual southern river. Known to the Indians as The Singing River, it divides into numerous passages as it meanders southward through the marshy savannah where salt water mixes with the muddy rainwaters coming down from the clay country to the north. In many ways, it is not unlike many other rivers of the south—the Tombigbee, the Chattahoochee, the Choc-

196

14

13. Numerous burrowing creatures live along the soft riverbanks. This track is made by a mole along the Suwannee.

14. The gaunt limpkin, with a distinct high-pitched call, is found in great numbers along the St. Johns and Oklawaha rivers, where it feeds exclusively on snails. The long hooked beak penetrates the shell from the open end and fishes out the little creature inside.

15. The river is always tearing away and building up; here are the remains of a great cypress tree the river has claimed at some time in the past and carried downstream.

16. Although the Suwannee has several stretches of riffles or rapids, most of the lower section of the river is placid with an almost imperceptible current.

15

16

tawhatchee, the Yazoo. But it is the only one having the legend of singing waters.

The singing sound, comparable to that made by a swarm of bees in flight, is best heard in late summer and early autumn, particularly in late evening. Fishermen who have heard it say it becomes amplified in the wells of their boats. And yet it has never been scientifically explained.

Although much of the Pascagoula is polluted by commercial interests, the state of Mississippi in 1976 took measures to preserve portions of it and the land along its route. The Pascagoula Tract, a 32,000-acre expanse of hardwood forest and bottomland straddling a thirty-five-mile stretch of the river, was set aside for recreation and wilderness. White-tailed deer, black bear, and game birds abound in the forest region, while fish thrive in the sandy-shored oxbow lakes. In this section, the river runs clean. Herman Murrah, a Mississippi state conservation officer, says it's so clean you can drink from it. "But," he adds jokingly, "it'll make your hair fall out."

17

198

19

17. White ibis nest by the hundreds along the upper Suwannee.

18. Along its upper stretches, the Suwannee is a blackwater river with white, sandy banks. The blackness of the water comes from tannin leached from decaying matter and from cypress trees.

19. A great brown pelican splashes down at the mouth of the Pascagoula River.

20. Many mushrooms are found along southern rivers, among them the Fat Pholiota, which may grow in the wound of a live tree or, more frequently, on dead trees. It is edible.

21. A winter sunset on the Suwannee.

22. Small oyster mushrooms grow from this water maple.

23. Carved into grotesque shapes by time and the tannin-stained waters of the Suwannee are these remnants of dead cypress trees.

24. Raindrops cascading from these oyster mushrooms along the Oklawaha will ultimately find their way into the river.

23

22

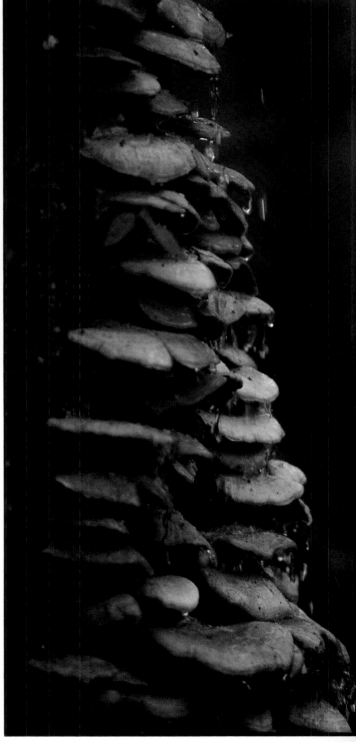

24

13

NEW ENGLAND RIVERS

The finest workers in stone
are not copper or steel tools, but the gentle
touches of air and water working
at their leisure with a liberal allowance of time.
—Henry David Thoreau/
A Week on the Concord and Merrimack Rivers

*1. White water and evergreen forest—the essence
of a wild New England river.*

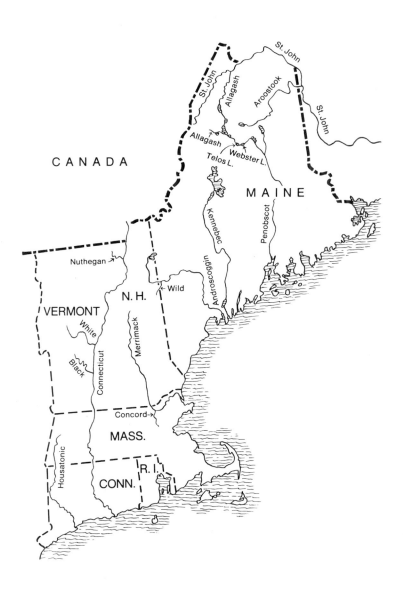

2. *Katahdin stream, flowing through Baxter State Park in northern Maine, was one of Thoreau's favorite places in New England. It has changed little since those days in the early 1800s.*

2

Spring is a great season to experience a New England river. Almost everywhere there is a fecund beauty. Rivulets from the high country search for another of their own kind to join in working their way to a brook, the brook to a creek, the creek to a river. As seeds held dormant throughout winter in the earth spring to life, pushing up the surface, the rivers burst, overflowing with the sweet, soothing sound of rushing water.

Spring comes first to the lower Connecticut, where the river empties into Long Island Sound, then marches up through New England all the way to the Allagash and the Penobscot. You can see the spring climbing, creeping, edging up the sides of the mountains, witness it in the trees as they bud and bloom and burst into leaf. It is a welcome sight, for the winters are harsh and long.

New England rivers are varied; they cannot all fit into the same category. Although there are a few rivers in New England that give one the impression of wildness—the Allagash in northern Maine, the Penobscot, and even the farmost upper reaches of the Connecticut—none are as natural as they were when Henry Thoreau stroked his way through the New England Wilds. None will likely ever be again. We can only imagine what they were like.

As New England rivers flow, the Connecticut is long—410 miles from the sandbar at its wide mouth on salty Long Island Sound to the sweet, small springs that spawn it in the New Hampshire hills just a few meters from the Canadian border. In that length it drops 2,650 feet. The Merrimack, immortalized by Thoreau's travels upon it, the Houstatonic, the Kennebec, and the Aroostook are only about one third as long. The Connecticut, slicing its way across the center of New England—Connecticut, Massachusetts, forming the boundary between New Hampshire and Vermont—might truthfully be acclaimed as the stream most representing this region. It is New England's river.

Sometimes it's difficult to trace a river, but not the Connecticut, bubbling from Scott's Bog, dimpling through four small New Hampshire lakes that bear its name, tumbling and cascading eight hundred feet in less than thirty miles to the town of Pittsburgh. The streams of the Presidential Range of the White Mountains add their contribution and the Connecticut is soon joined by Vermont's Nulhegan and the White and Black and Ottoqueechee and the West until it is a broad giant in the same league with the Ohio and the Missouri and other great rivers around the world. Draining some thirteen thousand square miles, the Connecticut is a noteworthy and sometimes temperamental stream.

The farther downstream you go, the more polluted the Connecticut beomes. It's cleaner today than it was yesterday or last year, thanks to a civic and future-minded organization called Connecticut River Watershed Council. Made up of businessmen and conservationists in the valley, and given sanction by such stalwart national figures as Connecticut's Sen. Abraham Riticoff and birdman Roger Tory Peterson, who lives along its banks, the council has made considerable strides since its formation in the early 1950s. But there is much yet to be done.

Consequently, the pristine qualities of the Connec-   **205** ticut's upper basin do not last long. In its midsection, great mills suck up the water and give it back dyed green or copper—the color of money. Nuclear and conventional power plants along the way, using the water in their cooling processes, raise the water temperature of the river enough to alter its ecosystem. A battery of seventeen dams not only block its flow but put an end to a once great Atlantic salmon run up the stream to natural spawning grounds.

For several years, the heated water from the Connecticut Yankee nuclear power plant at Haddam Neck has been discharged into the river, raising water surface temperatures by as much as ten to twelve degrees. The Essex Marine Laboratory, in a research project to determine the effects of this water upon fish, has been cautiously optimistic but admits it does have some detrimental effects. It influences the fish life directly, and also smaller forms of river life which, in turn, have an impact upon the larger forms. Thousands of white catfish and brown bullheads no longer winter in the bottom mud, as they have done for centuries, but instead, lie like cordwood in the unnaturally warm water. Although the fish feed more than they usually do, they show signs of emaciation.

The American shad has been a popular fish on this river for centuries. It makes a spawning run more dramatic than any other in New England, and some thirty-pound ones have been caught. Some begin spawning only thirty miles upstream from Long Island Sound, but others go farther, ascending the Enfield Dam via the sluiceway and being lifted over Holyoke Dam by an elevator. But then many of the newborn shad perish enroute back downstream to the Atlantic. They cannot get past Haddam Neck's thermal barrier, for the young fish are unable to survive in water ninety degrees Farenheit or above. And the nuclear power plant heats the river at this point even higher than that, particularly during late summer when natural water temperature is higher.

On the other hand, the lower Connecticut, despite heavy pollution, is vibrant with life. Fish, invertebrates, and microorganisms flourish in its depths. No complete inventory has ever been made of riverine life here, but one biologist says the lower reaches of the river are sometimes so glutted with marine life— alewife, bluejack herring, and young menhaden—that there is hardly room for water.

This part of New England along the Connecticut has had an interesting geological history. Formed by volcano and ice, rushing water, and the brilliant sun over eons, the land has known dinosaurs and mastodons. In fact, dinosaur tracks still may be seen to this day at Dinosaur State Park just south of Rocky Hill, Connecticut. The first tracks were discovered at Rocky Hill in 1966, then additional ones, until there are more than a thousand plainly visible today.

Volcanic activity in this area dates back about two hundred million years, when a fault occurred along what is now the eastern side of the lowland. As the range slowly appeared west of the fault line, rivers began to carve valleys in its flanks. The broken and decayed bedrock washed off the mountains and accumulated in broad alluvial fans.

3. Spring comes late along the Connecticut River, sometimes referred to as New England's River, for it stretches from Long Island Sound north to a place near the Canadian border.

4. Along the lower Connecticut, trees begin to fully leaf out by early May, while winter still lingers on in the river's upper reaches.

4

5. Phlox divaricata *pushes up through the wet leaves on the forest floor.*

6. *Cattails along the lower Connecticut begin to loose their seeds to the winds during the long winters. A single cattail head will seed thousands of new plants the following year.*

7. *Bogs and swamps throughout the mountainous areas of New England act as reservoirs, storing up the rainwater and gradually releasing it into the streams and underground flows.*

5

6

7

At three separate times, lava outpourings spread across what is today the Connecticut River basin and interrupted accumulations of sedimentary deposits. A layer of volcanic bombs and ash in the Holyoke region indicates the lava flow there was accompanied by violent volcanic activity, but elsewhere lava flowed gently from fissures in underlying rock. Later, the entire block of land known today as the Lowlands dropped like a great trapdoor. Another depression occured in the Pomperaug Valley near Woodbury, Connecticut; another in Cherry Brook Valley near Canton.

The Allagash Wilderness Waterway in northern Maine seems to me to be greatly overbilled as a wilderness river. It does provide something of a wilderness experience if you can survive the onrushing crowd, but is has been so altered by man that most purists come away feeling a little disappointed. In 1842 lumbermen decided to divert the flow from Telos and Chamberlain lakes from their normal northerly course into Canada and bend the river back south toward the profitable sawmills of Bangor. So they constructed a mile-long canal from Telos Lake east to Webster Lake to siphon Allagash headwaters into the Penobscot East Branch, thereby changing the character of both rivers.

Today, the river proper begins at the foot of Churchill Lake, where a dam impounds enough water during the spring runoff to keep the river navigable by canoe through the dry months of late summer. When you canoe the Allagash, you check in with the gatekeeper at the dam and he opens the gates enough to give you the kind of water you want for running the rapids downstream.

The Churchill Dam, built in 1968, replaced a series of rotted remnants of old logging dams. If it were not for the dam and the waters it impounds, however, the Allagash River might in fact dry up during dry periods, especially since a large part of its water is now diverted through the Penobscot.

Throughout the economic, legal, and political power struggle that culminated in the creation of the Allagash Wilderness Waterway, only one important voice raised the issue of restoring those waters diverted into the Penobscot back to the Allagash. Former Supreme Court Justice William O. Douglas, in his book *My Wilderness: East of Katahdin,* wrote:

Precious water, sorely needed if the Allagash is to be restored as the most wondrous canoe stream in the nation, runs needlessly into the East Fork (Penobscot) today.... We must move fast, if the whole chain of lakes and streams that make up the Allagash is to be preserved. Relics of old dams must be removed. The natural flow of Allagash waters must be restored. The tributaries of the Allagash must be protected by acquiring a wide corridor on each side of the waterway. This corridor must be free of roads, free of resorts, free of all marks of civilization. The Allagash must become and remain a roadless wilderness waterway. No more cutting of trees. No invasion of any kind.

Unfortunately, no one listened...the Allagash remains an artificial wilderness river.

There are wilderness places in New England, however. Most of them are in the high country that stretches north and east from the Berkshire and Taconic ranges of Connecticut and Massachusetts, through the Green Mountains of Vermont and the White Mountains of New Hampshire to the deep woods along the roof of Maine. They are known by such names as the Great Gulf, Caribou-Speckled Mountain, Moosehorn, Carr Mountain, Dry River-Rocky Branch, Kilkenny, and Wild River. One of the finest is the latter, located in the White Mountain National Forest of New Hampshire.

From the high country flow a myriad of streams converging in the broad floor of the valley to form Wild River. South of the stream is No-Ketchum Pond fed by drainage off Black Mountain. In the marshy grasslands along the stream are moose, beaver, and river otter. The land soon changes from marsh to a boreal forest of birch, balsam, and spruce—home for bobcat, black bear, fisher, and coyote. Showshoe hare, grouse, and even bald eagles also live here.

D. B. Wright, in his book *The Wild River Wilderness,* described the Wild River:

In an hour's time, during certain seasons or during one of the sudden and heavy rains that occur in the White Mountains, the river swells into a tremendous torrent—fierce, violent, and dangerous—acting as though it were its duty to protect from trespassers the wilderness it drains.

Thoreau would have been pleased such a stream still exists in the wild New England he loved so much.

8

8. Elm-pleur otus, *an edible mushroom, clings to the trunk of a tree along the Connecticut River.*

9. *The colors of maples, birch, and spruce soften the New England landscape in autumn.*

10. *The first warm days of spring bring forth the fiddlehead fern and a score of other plants bursting through the soft earthen banks of a New England stream.*

11. *The Connecticut is New England's longest and largest river, draining a good portion of New Hampshire, Vermont, Massachusetts, and Connecticut.*

12. *Along many New England streams in spring is found false hellebore, often mistaken for skunk cabbage; it seeks out low-lying areas where plenty of moisture is available.*

13. *Two mallard drakes and a hen feed from the waters along the West River, a tributary of the Connecticut.*

10

11

12

13

14

TO KILL A RIVER

The frog does not drink up
the pond in which he lives.
—American Indian Proverb

*1. The banks of the eroded Platte River in
Nebraska are stabilized with junk cars in plain
view of the highway.*

June 22, 1969, was like almost any other summer Sunday in Cleveland, Ohio. But by midafternoon something happened that would place Cleveland in an unfavorable news spotlight around the globe. First, Sunday strollers on downtown streets noticed black smoke billowing into the skies, but that wasn't anything to really get excited about. After all, smoke was a part of the city's environment. Fire engines soon were screaming through the streets, however, on one of the most unusual fire missions the city had ever experienced. The Cuyahoga River, flowing through the city's industrial area, was on fire.

The Cuyahoga had long been labeled the most polluted river in America, perhaps on earth. Now flames danced across the surface, crackling and leaping into the sky. Residents along the river were warned they might have to evacuate. The heavy putrid smoke was stifling. It was hard to believe that a river could catch fire...but anyone familiar with the stream wondered why it did not happen sooner.

There are many ways to kill a river. Burning is only one of them. Each year rivers are overwhelmed by silt from erosion, pollution from sewage, heat, chemicals, and industrial waste; their waters are choked by scores of dams and restrictive levees built in the name of progress. When we are not doing the dirty work ourselves as individuals, or collectively as communities, we finance such powerful agencies as the U.S. Army Corps of Engineers and the Bureau of Reclamation to do the job for us.

The average American city dweller, often insulated and out of touch with the natural environment, gives little thought to what happens to his body wastes once he has flushed the toilet. As far as he is concerned, this organic matter has magically disappeared from the face of the earth. Chances are, although it may have gone through a series of treatments to reduce its ultimate impact, it went into a river. And somewhere, downstream, someone drank the water.

The river, however, has remarkable self-cleansing qualities. Given the opportunity, and if not overburdened by too much waste, a river is more effective in cleaning its own waters than any filtering process engineered by man. The only trouble is that virtually all rivers near great cities are overburdened to the point where they have become simply open sewers transporting waste from one community to another. Already man's ignorance—or his indifference—relating to the matter is beginning to catch up to him.

Take New England's Merrimack River, for example. Henry Thoreau loved it because of its pristine qualities in the 1800s. By 1965 it was so thoroughly polluted that life within its waters was nearly nonexistent.

Once the Merrimack was the mother of a great fishing industry; today she smothers her children. Fish require water with substantial quantities of dissolved oxygen in order to live and propagate. But the oxygen readings on the entire Merrimack are below the level required by most species for propagation; in some places there is virtually no oxygen at all.

Untreated municipal sewage poured into the Merrimack in the 1960s contained huge quantities of

2. Creekbeds and riverbeds are a source of gravel in many parts of the country. The U.S. Army Corps of Engineers consistently dredges up the bottoms of rivers. Yet these stones play an important function in water purification, filtering out debris and harmful bacteria, providing shelter and seclusion for many smaller creatures.

3. The greatest deterrents to flood are dense forestlands and cover for the land. In the Pacific Northwest, flooding is seldom a problem because of the great forests with moss-clad floors which soak up the rains and prevent instant runoff.

4. Silting is another way man has allowed rivers to die. Here a stretch of channelized Rio Grande in New Mexico has virtually clogged its own assigned waterway.

5. The rechanneling of the Kissimmee River in south Florida by the Corps of Engineers caused such intense problems that the state of Florida currently is restoring it to its original meandering route through the marshes and swamps in order to give it the opportunity to clean its waters.

pathogenic organisms which could cause gastrointestinal diseases such as typhoid, dysentery, diarrhea, hepatitis, eye, ear, nose and throat disorders, skin infections, and possibly cancer. In the cleaner spots along the river, the spray thrown up over a motorboat's windshield will expose a passenger to dangerous numbers of bacteria.

A boater or swimmer on the Merrimack might come into contact with highly toxic chemicals and pesticides such as phenols, toxic wastes from metal-plating and chemical industries. Even cyanide—that chemical used in gas chamber executions at some prisons—was found in the Merrimack River. As early as 1887, the Massachusetts Department of Public Health, after running tests on the waters of the Merrimack, advised against its being used for drinking unless it was extensively treated. Today it has been improved, but still much remains to be done.

Something new is always turning up in river water contamination. A discovery in 1960 by Dr. Shih Lu Chang of the Robert A. Taft Sanitary Engineering Center in Cincinnati, Ohio, found that otherwise pure water from various American Rivers contains microscopic worms called nematodes. They can carry pathogenic bacteria and viruses. These nematodes are able to withstand chlorination and other severe treatment and act as protectors of the microorganisms attached to them. Thus a nematode can slip through a whole water purification system, carrying in its stomach, so to speak, the undigested bacteria. The worms are known to breed in sewage-disposal plants.

Nematode infestation was found in treated drinking water from the Mississippi in Illinois and Louisiana, from the Missouri River in Kansas, from the Potomac in Maryland, the Colorado in California, the Columbia, the Chattahoochee in Georgia, the Delaware in Pennsylvania, the Detroit River, the Rio Grande in Texas, the Merrimack, the Niagara, and the Tennessee.

The dumping of human sewage into our streams is mild compared to the problems created by other materials disposed of there. Chemical wastes without question pose the greatest threat, not only to our rivers but to humanity itself. A good case in point is the Kepone-laden waters of the James River in 1976. This roach poison, manufactured by a small plant in Hopewell, Virginia, first became an issue when workers at the plant suffered liver and brain damage. That was in the early part of 1976, but by late summer, traces of Kepone from that plant turned up in fish caught hundreds of miles away.

The U.S. Food & Drug Administration reported the pesticide residue was found in migratory fish caught by commercial fishermen in Chesapeake Bay (which the James flows into) and the Atlantic Ocean off the coast of Delaware, New Jersey, and New York. Fishing in the James River was closed for months shortly after it was found that Kepone had been dumped into the upper reaches of the stream.

One of the most vivid demonstrations of the results of river pollution occurred in Louisiana upon at least two occasions within a period of less than ten years. Up to 1962, Louisiana had so many brown pelicans that it was known as the Pelican State, and had adopted that as its slogan. The people of Louisiana were proud of their pelicans.

Then, suddenly, the brown pelicans disappeared. No longer were these graceful huge birds seen winging through the skies along the Gulf coasts. And everybody wondered why. After extensive studies, biologists determined the disappearance of the pelicans coincided with a massive fish kill at the mouth of the Mississippi River delta.

Further tests proved rather conclusively the kill was caused by pollutants suddenly flushed by heavy rains down the Mississippi from the farmlands up north. Attention initially was focused on the residual effects of DDT. But high concentrations of DDD, DDE, Dieldrin, and Endrin were also found. Louisiana decided to restock the birds, and in 1971 the first reestablished nesting colony was reported.

In the succeeding years, the brown pelican population in Louisiana seemed on its way back. U.S. Fish & Wildlife personnel worked diligently with Louisiana Wildlife and Fisheries people to create the most favorable conditions for the brown pelican, to protect them from harm, to supervise their every move. And it looked like it was going to work...until the spring of 1975. This time tragedy struck suddenly and without warning. Most of the birds disappeared within a few weeks. Again the Mississippi with its poison waters had dealt a lethal blow to the brown Pelican. Louisiana has since removed the nickname Pelican State from its auto license plates.

In 1975, Dr. Robert Harris of the Environmental Defense Fund found a definite correlation in statistics of cancer-inflicted persons in the cities taking their drinking water from the Mississippi and some of its tributaries. Cancer among people who drank this water occurred much more frequently than among people in other cities not using water from the river. And many of these chemicals have become a permanent part of the river, imbedding themselves in the bottom forever.

So it would seem that whenever we endanger the quality of our rivers, we indeed are doing great harm to our wildlife and ourselves. If this trend continues, it conceivably could come to the point within another twenty-five to thirty years that there would no longer be a single drop of uncontaminated water left on earth, certainly not in America's rivers.

Combine chemical and sewage pollutants with silt, eroded from America's mismanaged farmlands, add thermal pollution from atomic power plants and other facilities that use the rivers for cooling purposes, add radioactive wastes, and you have a complete picture of a dead river. Any life that can survive a stream environment such as man has created in New Jersey's Hackensack River would be a monster indeed, tolerant of everything, sensitive to nothing.

Dead rivers can be created by manipulation of water flow, too. Probably no better example exists than Florida's Kissimmee River, flowing from the vicinity of Orlando down to Lake Okeechobee, one of the largest natural lakes in the United States and the major source of water for the metropolitan areas of south Florida. In

6

6. *The river tugs at whatever is within reach. Nothing is safe. Once this barn and house stood a quarter mile away from the Ohio River in Indiana; today they have been undermined and parts of them swept away to the Mississippi, perhaps to the Gulf of Mexico.*

7. *When a river's banks are stripped of their protective tree and plant growth, the stream eats into the land, broadening its own channel, as the Ohio is doing here. It eventually will devour the farm buildings in the distance.*

8. *The rainwaters are a powerful force if the land is left barren. On this Kentucky farm, in only a few years, great scars are left upon the soil. In Georgia, dripping rainwater from a barn roof created a canyon in fewer than 100 years, only a moment in geologic time.*

its original state, the Kissimmee meandered for ninety miles or so through virtually virgin wilderness. Marshes and swamps lined its course, and when the river flooded, it fed these marshes and swamps. They, in turn, provided great habitat for all types of wildlife and in addition played a great ecological role in cleaning the waters of the river. Even the Corps of Engineers, in a report to Congress, stated: "The water of the Kissimmee River is of the best quality to be found in southeastern Florida." But that was before the Corps moved in to make things even better.

Just eight years later, the pollutants poured into Lake Okeechobee by the Kissimmee reached such high levels that the water was dangerous for human use. The reason: the Corps of Engineers had, as a means of making the river more efficient, channelized it into a straight ditch, 150 to 200 feet wide and 30 feet deep, which eliminated the inconvenience of seasonal high water. Farmers were pleased; so were the developers and municipal authorities in and around Orlando, where the economy and population were being spurred by the new Disney World complex.

The Kissimmee River no longer meandered anywhere. There were no trees along its banks, nor marshes, nor swamps. The waters, exposed to the direct sun, were too hot to sustain some types of aquatic life. There were no protective coves or places to permit eddies. The Kissimmee River, once nationally known for its huge largemouth bass, now became a dead, sterile ditch good for only one thing—the transportation of water. Since it tolerated virtually no life, it had no cleaning qualities, and the water, now filled with pollutants from sewage, pesticides from orange groves, and cropland runoff, industrial wastes from Orlando and other sites, went directly into Lake Okeechobee.

In 1977 the Florida legislature voted to correct the situation. The Kissimmee River would be returned, insofar as possible, to its original state. This would cost the taxpayers of Florida some $30 million—an expensive lesson that it's not nice to fool with Mother Nature.

There is hope for the Kissimmee, and there is hope for many of America's rivers, for with corrective action they can still be salvaged. The Willamette River, a tributary of the Columbia in Oregon, is an excellent example of a river being reborn. Today it is one of the cleanest rivers in the nation; in 1960 it was one of the filthiest. Municipalities piped raw sewage into it. Pulp and paper mills added wood residues and strong chemicals. Food processors donated all their leftovers. As the bacteria level rose, oxygen levels dropped—to near zero in some places. Fish died, and the threat of disease put a stop to safe swimming. Rafts of sunken sludge, surfacing in the heat of summer, discouraged water skiing and took the pleasure out of boating. The river had become an eyesore, and nobody wanted to go near it. It was best to look the other way.

First to come to the rescue of the river were fishermen and conservationists. Among them was Tom McCall, a popular television newscaster who had political aspirations. In 1961, McCall produced a documentary film that showed just how rotten the river had become. It was a shocker. Some polluters threatened to

9, 10. Dams do far more damage than man realizes to the river's intricate ecosystem. They slow the current, allowing it to drop its silt, covering its bottom constantly and killing off much life that exists there. By raising the water level, the dams create new erosion and limit the cleansing action of the stream. Some, such as the one at Flaming Gorge, Utah (top) on the Green River, harness the stream for electricity and recreation; the purposes of the one on the Ohio (bottom) are flood control and navigation aid.

9

10

sue, but they soon backed down. Just five years later, McCall ran for governor on a cleanup platform and won handily.

The result of McCall's efforts was a reasonable and economically feasible program to improve the Willamette. It reduced waste discharge into the river by ninety percent, increased the number of migratory salmon, native trout, and other game fish, boosted overall water quality to meet strict state and federal standards, and made the river safe again for all water sports including swimming. Surprisingly, the state has not had to bring court action against a single violator, and only one small company chose to shut down rather than conform to the stringent new legislation. American Can and other major industrial users have shown their support for the highly ambitious Greenway program, which proposes eventually to edge the river with a nearly continuous strip of public land.

Though Tom McCall is no longer governor, Oregon today is known as one of the most environmentally conscious states in America. The Department of Environmental Quality has great power to levy fines against air and water polluters. It encourages industries to clean up by giving tax credits to those which install antipollution equipment. And it awards seals that can be displayed on the merchandise of companies that take outstanding steps against pollution.

Limits have been set on noise pollution, too, including the noise level in the wilderness areas. A Scenic Waterways System has the power to protect several Oregon rivers from dams and uncontrolled development along the shore.

To protect the countryside and rivers from litter, Oregon passed a law which specifies all carbonated soft drink and malt beverage bottles and cans must be sold with a deposit. The same law forbids the sale of cans with pull-tab openers.

And Oregon is discouraging the use of automobile as a means of transportaton. The Legislature set aside one percent of all state and highway funds to install bicycle and foot trails along existing and planned roads. A good many miles of bike trails are already constructed. And one might say it all began with the atmosphere created by the cleanup of the Willamette River. Oregonians can indeed be proud of the task they undertook and the results obtained. It provides positive proof to the rest of the nation that something can be done about the plight of our rivers if only we are willing to put forth the effort and pay the price to do it. Tomorrow may be too late.

11

11. *The Willamette River in Oregon is perhaps the country's best example of a river given new birth. Even though it is heavily industrialized along much of its course, as shown here by this logging and papermill operation, citizens of Oregon brought about a remarkable clean-up to transform the river from one of the filthiest in the West.*

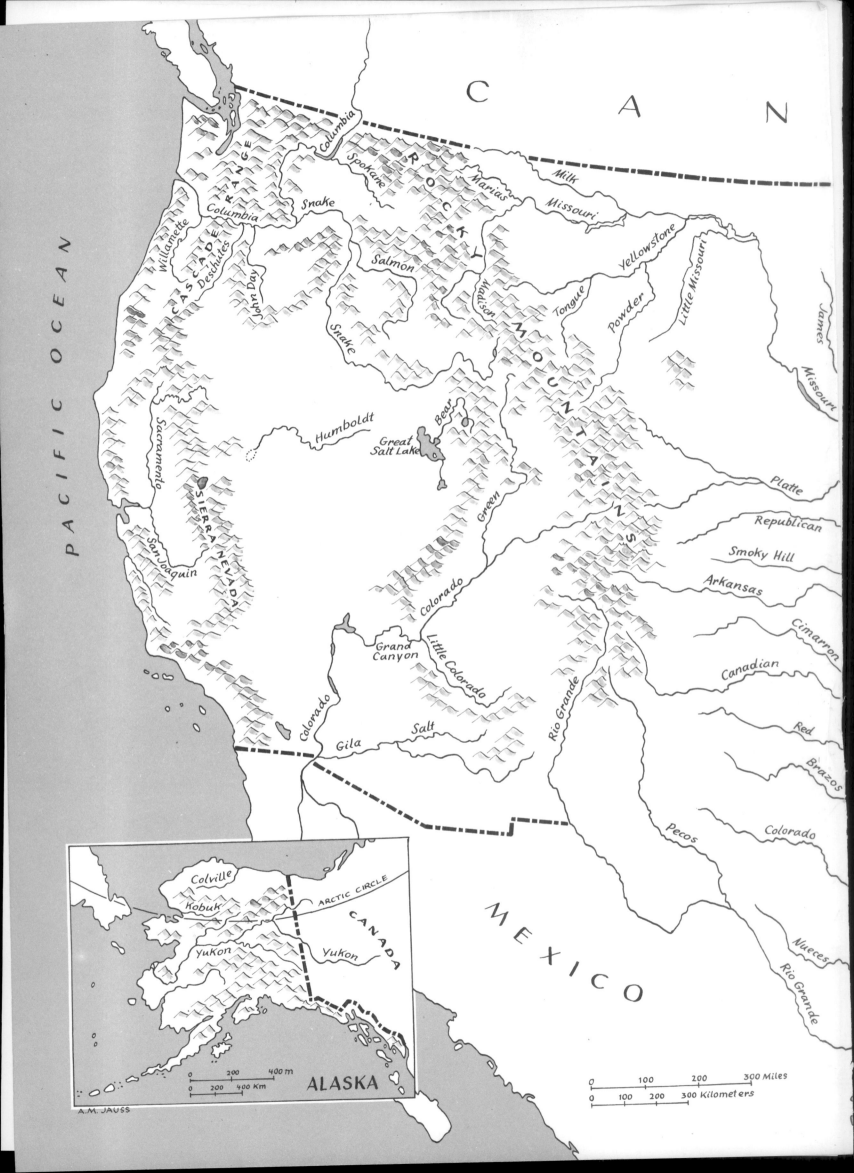

O C E A N

PACIFIC OCEAN

CASCADE RANGE

Columbia

Willamette
Columbia
Deschutes
John Day

Snake

Spokane

ROCKY

Marias

Milk

Missouri

Salmon

Snake

Madison

Yellowstone

Tongue

Powder

Little Missouri

James

Missouri

Sacramento

Humboldt

Great
Salt Lake

Bear

Green

MOUNTAINS

Platte

Republican

SIERRA NEVADA

San Joaquin

Smoky Hill

Arkansas

Colorado

Cimarron

Grand
Canyon

Little Colorado

Canadian

Colorado

Gila

Salt

Rio Grande

Red

Brazos

Pecos

Colorado

MEXICO

Nueces

Rio Grande

Colville

Kobuk

Yukon

ARCTIC CIRCLE

CANADA

Yukon

ALASKA

200   400 m
0
200   400 Km

A.M. JAUSS

0   100   200   300 Miles

0   100   200   300 Kilometers